W9-CPY-494

The Overseas Assignment:
A Professional's Guide
for Working in
Developing Countries

The Overseas Assignment: A Professional's Guide for Working in Developing Countries

by

C.N. Weller, Jr.

PENNWELL PUBLISHING COMPANY
TULSA, OKLAHOMA

Dedication

Rianty Handojo

. . . a world class executive secretary by any standard

Contents

Preface   xi

Acknowledgements   xv

Introduction   xvii

Chapter   1   The Employment Agreement Letter   1

Chapter   2   Conditions of Employment   9

Duration of employment, 9 • Family status, 9 • Transportation from and return to point of origin, 9 • Schedule of payments to employee, 10 • Employee's personal income taxes, 11 • Retirement and other social benefits, 13 • Visas, work permits and similar documents, 14 • Temporary accommodations when arriving and departing, 16 • Employee's permanent residence, 18 • Repairs to employee's residence, 19 • Security guard service, 21 • Dependent schooling, 24 • Employee's and covered dependent's personal effects, 25 • Insurance coverage for employee's personal effects, 29 • Automobiles, 29 • Vacations, 32 • Short leave, 33 • Transportation during vacations and short leave, 36 • Medical insurance, 37 • Life insurance, 37 • Personal accident insurance, 38 • Death or injury, 38 • Business expenses, 39 • Social and business clubs, 43 • Use of telephones, 43 • Termination due to political or civil unrest, 46 • Termination by employer, 47 • Termination by employee, 48 • Statements to the media, 49 • Extension of the agreement, 50 • Entire agreement, 50 • Interpretation, 51 • Compliance with law, 51 • Clarifications, 52

Chapter   3   Attachment I: Medical Examinations, Insurance, and Medical Records   53

Initial and annual medical examinations, 53 • Immunization, 54 • Medical examinations and the employer's rights, 55 • Covered dependent failure of medical examination, 55 • Location of examining clinic, 56 • Time and compensation during medical examinations, 57 • Medical insurance, 57 • Medical records to be kept confidential, 60 • Locally available medical care, 60 • Getting involved ensures good health, 61 • Hygiene and the household staff, 65 • Getting approvals for emergency medical evacuation, 66 • Health care for the household staff, 67 • Being cautious about lab work and reports, 68 • Nursing care for the patient, 69

Chapter   4   Attachment II: Employee's Instruction to Payroll   71

Moving funds as quickly and safely as possible, 73 • Other reasons for delays in the transfer of funds, 74

Chapter   5   Attachment III: Insurance   77

Term life insurance, 77 • Accidental death and dismemberment insurance, 77 • Loss of income insurance, 78 • Workman's compensation insurance, 78 • Personal effects insurance, 78 • General notes, 79 • Workmans' compensation for household staff, 80 • Liability insurance, 80 • Automobile insurance, 80 • Verification of beneficiary, 81 • Finding someone to turn to in case of need, 82

Chapter   6   Attachment IV: Guide for Selecting Employee's Residence   83

General notes, 83 • Master bedroom and bath, 85 • Additional bedrooms and baths, 85 • Study or office, 85 • Television and recreation room, 85 • Living room, 85 • Dining room, 86 • Kitchens, 86 • Pantry, 86 • Laundry, 86 • Kitchen and laundry appliances and cabinets, 86 • Staff accommodations, 87 • Garage, 87 • Store room, 87 • Doors, general, 87 • Window screens, 88 • Curtains and drapes, 88 • Burglar bars, 88 • Carpets, 88 • Furniture, 88 • Perimeter wall and exterior security, 89 • The roof, 89 • Telephone system, 89 • Intercom system, 90 • Security alarm system, 90 • Electrical system, general, 90 • Lighting, general, 91 • Exterior floodlighting, 91 • Air conditioning, 91 • Water system, 92 • Hot water system, 93 • Sanitary sewer and drains, 93 • Swimming pool, 93 • Swimming pool bath and toilet, 94 • Pest control, 94

Chapter   7   Attachment V: Employee's Job Description   95

Employee's title or position, 95 • Department to which employee is assigned, 95 • Executive memo authorizing position, 95 • Date of executive memo, 96 • Name and title of person employee reports to, 96 • Employee's required background, 96 • Employee's authority, 97 • Limits of authority, 98 • Overlapping and coordinating functions, 99 • Schedule for employment, 99 • Review of employee's performance, 100 • Schedule of pay, bonus, and Conditions reviews, 100 • Miscellaneous, 100

Chapter 8 Attachment VI: General Requirements for Secretaries   103
Skills, 103 • Personality and appearance, 106 • Required background, 108 • Specific authority, 108

Chapter 9 Evaluation of Terms and Conditions   109

Chapter 10 Sources of Information for the Employee   125

Chapter 11 Matchmaking or Back to Basics   129
Fundamentals, 129 • The employee's "body of knowledge", 130 • Resources, 130 • Time, 131 • Delegation of authority, 132 • Leadership, 133 • Performance measurement, 134 • Employee's understanding of his or her assignment, 137 • A closing comment, 137

Preface

Most people would agree it ludicrous for an employer in a developing country to hire an employee from a developed country, often at substantial cost, only to find later that flaws in the relationship develop which reduce the employee's effectiveness in his or her job. This is often the result of an early misunderstanding of each party's intentions and view of the relationship. It may also be fueled by the employee's romantic concept of such employment, especially if he or she has never worked in a developing country (or overseas at all). Unfortunately, this situation is common in both indigenous and multinational organizations in developing countries, and it is generally the result of poor or incomplete communications between the parties during pre-employment (or assignment) discussions.

If the employer is a company domiciled in a developing country, there will be differences in culture and language that may and often do lead to misunderstandings. Although such an employer may speak the employee's language perfectly (it isn't usually the other way around), he may not interpret the meaning of words and concepts in the same way. Avoiding these and other similar difficulties is what this book is about.

The purpose of this book is to improve communications and understanding between employers and expatriate employees by presenting and discussing key aspects of employment in overseas assignments, especially in developing countries, that should be thoroughly understood and agreed to in writing before the employee accepts or is sent to such an assignment. The content is generic and not meant to be critical of anyone or any country. The goal is for employers and employees to be better informed of the various aspects of such employment so that they will (hopefully) avoid many of the pitfalls that can otherwise detract from the relationship. In so doing, they both can realize the benefits from the experience.

Employment in a developing country environment was chosen since such assignments will generally be the most difficult for the newly arrived employee and his or her family (if he or she has one). In addition, the majority of language used in this book implies that the employer's company is domiciled in a developing country. Again, this is to recognize the additional factors that should be considered before offering or accepting such employment.

The type of employee contemplated is a man or woman in a craft, supervisory, management, or executive position, with spouse and school-aged children. The individual might be in any commercial or technical field and from any developed nation. The term *he* is used as a convenience only when describing the employee and is not intended to slight the female gender, although both he and she are also used. The reader will also see the terms employee or expatirate employee, which are used to identify the person being hired for (or assigned to) a job in a developing country. At one time the term expatriate referred to a person who had fled his country of origin. In more recent times, it is commonly used to describe any person working in a foreign land, although the original meaning may still apply.

As mentioned in the Acknowledgements, this book originated as a collection of notes for the author's own use. While the terms and conditions generally parallel those offered by multinational companies for their married expatriate employees, the terminology used in multinational company agreements typically contain more legalese, involve "if" conditions, and, in general, are more complicated. Such terminology is not conducive to understanding and could make communications between a developing country employer and the expatriate employee more difficult. Therefore, much of the original language has been retained, which should make the concepts presented here easier for the layman (such as the author) to understand. Of particular importance is achieving a simple and clear understanding of the *net* amount that the expatriate employee will be paid.

The suggestions contained in this book have been constructed around the assumption that both the employer and employee are principled, fair, and reasonable people, are entering into the relationship intending to be responsible for the business and welfare of the other party, and that neither have hidden agendas. These suggestions also apply to single status employees except for those parts which obviously relate to the expatriate employee's dependents.

While all knowledge can improve an individual's marketability, this book is not intended to explain how the employee should dress, how to prepare a professional resume, or the fundamentals of acceptable social behavior. The assumption is that any employee interested in work in a developing country will already be accomplished in these areas and additionally have educated him or herself on the history and customs, (and maybe even the language) of the country. The employer expects that a *professional* will not only know his or her business, but will also be able to work in an organized, understandable, and accountable manner; remain friendly with those with whom he or she must work, and be able to communicate and train native staff.

From the standpoint of an employer in a developing country, he will often have an advantage in the broad areas of communications and knowledge of other countries, since he will likely be well traveled, educated in one of the western countries, and speak several languages besides his own native tongue. He may even know more about the history and have visited more parts of the expatriate employee's home country than the employee! However, he is also a minority in his own nation because few of his countrymen have such opportunities.

Herein lies the paradox with which an employer must deal. He has seen and admires the technical advances and much of the life-style of the developed countries. He wants a better life, first for himself and his immediate family and relatives, then for his fellow countrymen. However, he is not always able to find enough countrymen that have the same education and experience that he has and are willing to work for his company (rather than manage their own businesses). Therefore, he turns to the expatriate employee who he hopes to hire on a temporary basis to help train native employees and often to act as a bridge or communications link between his organization and multinational companies operating in his country.

Developing countries need the transfer of knowledge required to help solve economic and social problems. The term *transfer* implies communications. Communications is intended to lead to understanding and self- reliance. This book seeks to bring about a better understanding between employers and prospective expatriate employees upon which mutual trust can be developed. Where trust exists a mutually beneficial relationship can be built.

Although the target of this book is employment situations in developing countries, the section entitled "Matchmaking or Back to Basics," Attachment V "Employee's Job Description," Attachment VI "General Requirements for Secretaries," and "Evaluation of Terms and Conditions" can be used as guides for domestic employment as well.

As the case with most *guides*, most of the suggestions contained in the employment agreement letter and conditions of employment are in the public domain in one form or another, and they are available to anyone who wants to take the time to do the research and go to the expense of putting it all together. What is not in the public domain is the author's personal experience while living and working outside his country of origin in both developing and developed countries. This experience was used in preparing the Forward, Introduction, Attachments I through VI, Evaluation of Terms and Conditions, Matchmaking or Back to Basics, and the comments as well as *putting it all together*. While some of the experiences mentioned in the book are the author's own, others have been passed on to the author by word of mouth and are believed to represent the experience related, although the venue and other aspects have been modified in order to protect the privacy of the person(s) involved. The author has not had personal contact with the persons involved in these experiences and makes no guarantee as to their accuracy.

In closing, it is important to emphasize that this book was developed from notes collected for my own use. I am not and do not represent myself to be an attorney nor are the contents offered as professional legal advice. This book should only be used as a *guide* in obtaining a better understanding of the complexity of expatriate employment.

Anyone considering an employment situation in a developing country, whether employer or expatriate employee, should seek the advice of an attorney, preferably one with experience with employment contracts in developing countries; a major international accounting firm which has offices in the specific country, and an insurance consultant. Neither the author nor the publisher assume any liability for the completeness or the accuracy of the information contained herein or use of the contents in whole or in part. Any adaptation of this book is made at the sole discretion and risk of the user.

Acknowledgements

This book began as a collection of notes for my own personal use in negotiating contracts for overseas employment. It never occurred to me to develop these into a book until it was suggested by a friend. At the time we were living in a developing country, and my wife and I were attending a dinner at Clare McMahon's house. Clare was an Australian Trade Commissioner. The discussion turned to expatriate employment in developing countries and the difficulties that it entails. Someone said that a guide on the subject would be useful for native employers, as well as for expatriate employees. I mentioned the notes I had collected. Clare asked to read these which she did over the next several weeks. She said my notes contained the essentials that should be considered by both parties before entering into an employment agreement and that I should put them in book form. That was a number of years and innumerable revisions ago.

Since Clare's initial encouragement, several other people have lent their time, experience, and support on the long road to publication. The first draft was reviewed by Darrell Korman, a long-time friend who, with his wife, Carol, has spent most of his engineering career on overseas assignments, primarily in developing countries and on several continents. Others have reviewed more recent drafts and offered comments, suggestions, and much appreciated advice. These include Judy Clark, editorial consultant and (formally) editor of *Pipeline Digest*, Ian M. Koenig, PMP and vice president of Quality IS Projects, Donna J. Harvey, a regional sales director of International SOS Assistance, Inc., and our good friend and neighbor, Ann Anderson, teacher and artist extraordinaire.

Needless to say, a book such as this must be reviewed by an attorney with firsthand international experience. This task was performed by Richard F. Wornson of Wornson & Commiskey. I first met Dick in a developing country where he was a member of our employer's negotiating team. More recently, attorneys Bobbit Noel and Leslie Clark of Vinson & Elkins LLP have provided valuable advice on contracts and intellectual properties.

I also want to mention Sue Rhodes Sesso, acquisitions editor and Marla M. Patterson, petroleum editor at PennWell Publishing whose support, encouragement, and constructive criticism is much appreciated.

To all of the above, many thanks.

Nelson Weller

Introduction

Not many people from developed nations work outside their own country. Of those who do, most work in other developed nations and a small percentage work in developing nations. Of those who do work in developing nations, the majority work for locally registered units of multinational companies and very few work directly for companies indigenous to that country. While the last two situations may appear to be similar, working for a unit of a multinational in a developing country will not be the same as being employed by a wholly owned and operated indigenous company.

To begin, it is rare that such companies have offices or significant ties to organizations in the expatriate employee's home country. As a result, the employee will not likely have a corporate communications link for such items as mail, emergency messages, spare parts expediting for appliances and similar support that is more likely to be considered routine in multinational companies. An insurance package often has to be purchased solely for the employee's and dependent's coverage, since few such companies normally provide it for their indigenous employees. The employee may have to be his or her own insurance department, since no one else in the company is familiar with the forms to be submitted for claims or other requirements.

Other differences are often found in the management style and method, decision-making process, the pace at which work is accomplished, in business customs, internal communications, planning, and in the general efficiency of the company. To the uninitiated, the many differences can be overwhelming. The term "culture shock" is often used to describe the impact of being suddenly immersed in an unfamiliar society. The employee going to work for an indigenous company in a developing country can expect to undergo two such experiences. One experience is related to the society in general, and the other experience is related to the business methods and practices of the new employer and other local companies with which the expatriate employee comes into contact.

As mentioned in the Preface, a main reason why employers in developing nations hire expatriate employees is to gain the knowledge needed to advance their businesses. On the other hand, why do expatriate employees seek (or accept) assignments in developing countries? In the majority of cases the primary purpose is to increase annual savings. In addition, the employee may want to experience overseas travel and learn more about other cultures.

Whatever the employer's and employee's expectations, they will not end up at odds if ideas are candidly shared and contemplated over some reasonable period of time, if a well thought out agreement negotiated and committed to paper, and if little assumed by either party. While this concept is generally true in any job, in a hiring situation in a developing country the employee and the employer need to go into a lot more detail before entering into an employment agreement. The reason is that basic assumptions and the rules of the game are often substantially different, or interpreted differently, in developing nations. The employer may recognize this and assume that the employee does also. However, it is unlikely that the expatriate employee, especially if he or she has no prior experience in the country (or overseas at all), will understand the differences. This results in too much being assumed.

There are often differences in the way legal matters are viewed by societies in developing countries as well. For example, while most developed countries have very specific laws that protect the rights of the Employee (whether indigenous or expatriate), the same is not always true in all developing countries.

This is not to say that there are not laws in these countries similar to those in developed countries; rather, that the predominance of protection will probably be given the employer in the interpretation of these laws. This is especially so where a general, nonspecific agreement exists between the parties. But even where a specific agreement does exist, the expatriate employee may not be able to obtain a fair and impartial judgment in some developing countries, if he or she needs to resort to legal action. As with all matters of law, the situation described will vary from country to country and over time. In any case, the employee needs to be informed about the level of risk associated with employment contracts in the country before accepting the job.

Probably the best way for the expatriate employee to achieve this is through feedback from a trusted acquaintance who has experience in the country. If the acquaintance can also recommend a lawyer in the country who is willing to be candid about such matters, so much the better. The point is that no useful purpose will be served by either the employer or employee finding themselves in a situation where there is an ongoing interpretation of the terms of employment, or where the relationship is on the verge of legal action. To avoid such pitfalls, there has to be extra attention given to employment details beforehand so that a clear understanding and mutual trust evolves that will allow both parties to receive what each expects from the experience.

The need to give extra attention to details of the proposed employment conditions is also related to cultural differences; more specifically, it relates to the differences in social and business mentality. In the first place, clever and aggressive bargaining is a way of life in developing countries. It permeates every aspect of daily activities. No one shopping in a market, for example, would consider paying the price first asked for the goods or services desired.

In more serious matters (as a general rule) where no written agreement exists, a disagreement may be resolved in favor of the party perceived to have the higher social or political status. Even where a written agreement exists, the employer may feel that he should get some *extra* concession from the expatriate employee due to his perception that he has the greater *status*. In other words, a written agreement is often looked upon as simply a "basis" for further negotiations.

The employer in a developing country may concentrate more on what is left out than what is included in an agreement. He is likely to look upon an understanding quite opposite from the view of the expatriate employee, while zeroing in on what he doesn't have to do or what is not absolutely clear in the agreement. The fact that this approach may appear to be negative to the expatriate, and affect the relationship and eventually the effectiveness, efficiency, and motivation of the employee, is still not generally recognized in developing countries.

This is further complicated by the reaction often displayed concerning those items that are spelled out in detail in the agreement, which is to simply ignore them. For example, the employment agreement may call for provision of a secretary for the expatriate employee. The employee may assume that it is obvious that he or she cannot perform efficiently without this position being filled (the sooner the better). However, weeks may pass without any action on the part of the employer to provide candidates for interview, despite constant reminders from the employee. The candidates finally interviewed may all be related to various executives or other employees within the company and have few of the needed skills. It is easy to see that frustration can soon set in. When the exasperation level reaches the upper tolerance point, the employee finally decides to bypass the employer's organization and find his or her own secretary. Incidentally, one source always worth checking is through the *executive services* offices of major hotels nearby.

In another example, during the job interview the employee may be shown a private office and advised that when he or she reports for work similar facilities will be furnished. However, when the employee returns he or she is told that there had been some shuffling in administrative personnel after the visit and that the office is not yet available. In the meantime, the employee is asked to sit behind a tiny desk in a large (and often noisy) office crowded with people. Months may go by without any *real* effort made by the employer to provide the "assumed" facilities. When the matter finally gets to the critical stage in the relationship, the employer may question why the employee needs such special facilities when he or she was agreeable to accepting the desk in the large and noisy office after first arriving. In other words, there is a tendency for temporary (and unacceptable) solutions to become permanent.

The employment agreement will typically require that the employer provide all maintenance for the employee's home and appliances. However, when a need arises, little or no effort is made to make repairs. It is easy to visualize the effect of days or weeks without telephone service, air-conditioning, the clothes dryer or running water, and a leaking roof on the attitude of the employee and family. Yet, these types of problems tend to be the rule rather than the exception and eventually take their toll in the business relationship.

The bottom line is that any agreement is only as good as the integrity of the parties that put it together. On this subject my grandfather had a saying that, "Any two adults who felt they were smart enough and willing to enter into a *verbal* agreement should have no objection or difficulty in putting their understanding in writing." I would add with the help of a lawyer, accountant, and insurance specialist. He went on to say that, "If one of the parties objected to spelling out the terms in writing, it was a good sign that he never intended to fulfill his part of the bargain in the first place."

This concept was true in my grandfather's time, and it is just as true today. Having said this, one must recognize that there is no substitute for the employer and employee getting to know each other and developing a sense of the other person's character. If a feeling of trust evolves and both are willing to reduce their understanding to writing, then one can expect that there is reasonable chance for mutual satisfaction. If the situation doesn't "feel" right, then the relationship will probably not have much chance of success, no matter how much paperwork or advice in which the parties have invested.

This Introduction is followed by a typical employment agreement. There are eight parts to the employment agreement. These are:

- The employment agreement letter
- The conditions of employment
- Chapter 1 through 6

Since this was originally prepared for my own use in negotiating my own overseas employment agreements the language used is the everyday variety and should be easily understood. The reader's attorney will probably incorporate a number of modifications to fit the particular employment circumstances and as his own experience in preparing employment agreements may dictate. Note that the term "employee" appearing in these documents is synonymous with the term "expatriate."

The need for certain paragraphs or sentences may not be clear. Anticipating this, comments and examples are included where it was felt appropriate. These are intended to provide background and a better understanding of the importance of specific paragraphs. It is recognized that employers in developing countries who have previously hired expatriates and expatriates with previous experience in such countries will have a better understanding and may decide to skip the comments, and refer to them only where appropriate.

It is suggested that expatriates who have not worked in a developing country (or overseas at all) review this material with someone who has lived and worked in that country.

As mentioned in the Preface, the expatriate employee should always obtain the services of a lawyer, accountant, and insurance advisor prior to entering into an agreement for overseas employment.

The employment agreement letter, conditions of employment, and Chapters 1 through 6 are *generic* and can't possibly cover all of the employment situations. These documents (without the commentary) are in individual files in ASCII format on the floppy disk that comes with the book. The files can be copied to a hard drive and modified by most word processing programs to address specific employment situations.

1

The Employment
Agreement Letter

(Insert Employer's Company Name)
(Employer's Address)
(Employer's City, Province, and Country)

EMPLOYMENT AGREEMENT LETTER

This agreement is made this _____ day of _____, 19____ between **(employer's company name)**, (hereinafter referred to as "employer"), a **(here insert the type of company)** formed under the laws of the **(form of government)** of **(country)**, and Mr/Mrs/Miss/Ms **(here insert expatriate's name)** (hereinafter referred to as "employee").

Employer employs the employee, and employee agrees to accept employment in accordance with the following terms and conditions:

1. Employee's position or title: _____

2. Title of person to whom employee shall report: _____

3. Employee's monthly base salary shall be: US $ _____

4. Employee's monthly bonus shall be: US $ _____ per month or, US $ _____ per year of employment.

5. The covered dependents of employee under this agreement are as follows: *

	Name	Age	Sex
Spouse:	_____	____	____
Child:	_____	____	____

* Use additional sheet if required

Child: _____   _____ _____

Child: _____   _____ _____

Other: _____   _____ _____**

** Specify relationship

6. Employee's point of origin: **(address, city, state, postal code)**

7. Employee's country of origin: _____

8. The duration of this agreement shall be _____ months.

9. Employee's permanent residence place while under the agreement shall be: **(where expatriate will be living)**

10. The commencement date of this agreement shall be: _____

11. Employer is to notify the employee's next of kin shown below in case of emergency:

Name: _____

Relationship: _____

Address: _____

Phone: _____

12. Employee's normal work schedule shall be:

(provide details)

13. Employee shall take short leave at one of the following locations:

(provide details)

14. The documents entitled "conditions of employment" and "attachments" "I" through "VI" are attached and incorporated herein by this reference. Employee has read the conditions of employment and attachments I through VI. Both parties have signified their agreement to the conditions of employment and attachments I through VI and this employment agreement letter (all of which are hereinafter referred to as the "agreement") by *initialing each page* and signing below.

This agreement has been read, is understood, and is accepted by employee and employer as indicated by their signatures below:

Employee	**Employer**
Signature: _____	Signature: _____
Name (print or type): _____	Title: _____
Date: _____	Date: _____

Note

Each party is to receive an *original*, and each *original* is signed by both parties. Very often contracts will not be valid unless the signatures are made over duty stamps. In other words, the employee signs over a duty stamp on the *original* that the employer is to keep; the employer signs over a duty stamp on the *original* that the employee is to keep. Also, verify that the duty stamps used are the correct ones for the *type* and *value* of the contract.

What Is the Purpose of the Employment Letter?

The purpose of this document is to gather essential data in a short form rather than have these details inserted in sentences throughout the other parts of the agreement. This is convenient for the employer, since he can use the same conditions of employment and attachments for each employee and fill in the blanks in the employment agreement letter as appropriate to each employee. Consolidating essential information in this way also makes it easier for both the employer and employee to review compensation and find emergency information, if required.

The Job Title and Necessity
for Management Cooperation

In addition to providing the employee with a job title that relates to the work to be performed, the employer must insure that the employee receives full cooperation from other company management and staff.

The preferred method of achieving this is for the employer to introduce the employee to the staff during negotiations (where these are being conducted in the employer's home offices) and, when an agreement has been reached, prepare and circulate a memo explaining in more detail the employee's background and what his or her function will be. The memo should include at least the date the employee reported to work, the name of the senior manager acting as the employee's sponsor or mentor, the employee's immediate supervisor, a brief description of the purpose of his or her hiring (possibly some comments about the staff who will be reporting to the employee), and (most importantly) specific language making it plain that company management expects the full cooperation of company management and other employees in making the work for which the employee was employed a success. If the employee is to interface with the company's clients, the employer should send a letter of introduction to each client (or supplier, etc.) that includes a description of the part the employee will play in the company.

Needless to say, the employee also has to do his or her part for such an introduction to have meaning and for the assignment to be effective. Although the employee may be assigned to a very high position in the employer's organization and have a glowing introduction, he or she should be aware of the importance of *face* in some societies. While the employee will be providing technology transfer to other employees, maybe even senior members of the management, such communications should be structured in a way that does not imply that the employee is somehow *superior* or by a method or manner of communications that may be taken as lecturing, belittling, condescending, or arrogant as viewed in *that* society. Any actions that detract from the other person's image or position of authority should be avoided. For example, correcting an employee directly and without regard for the personal feelings of the employee is common in some developed countries. Such actions would be considered rude in many developing countries, even if the situation concerned a serious matter.

Also, in at least one society it is not good form to bring problems directly to the attention of the company president, as one might in a developed country. It is more appropriate to discuss the matter privately (and politely) with a close relative, perhaps his or her older brother or sister. That person then discusses the matter with their father, who chooses an appropriate time and place to bring the problem to the attention of the company president. Eventually, the problem will be resolved, sometimes without the employee knowing how.

One mistake many employees make on first arrival in a developing country is assuming they will be able to follow the same procedures and philosophies used in their country of origin in their new assignment. For example, if a local contractor isn't performing and one-on-one discussions haven't solved the problem, it still may be inadvisable to abruptly terminate the contract, either verbally or in writing. Protracted negotiations are often required and probably best left to the employer's indigenous staff. The reason, again, is *face*. Having a contract summarily canceled—a common practice in developed countries—is often taken as a public insult because it indicates that the terminated party is incompetent, even if that isn't the reason. In at least one such case the offended party had strong political ties and had the expatriate president and another top expatriate official with a multinational company arrested and detained at the local police station. The matter was eventually settled but required intervention by some very important persons and weeks of negotiations. A substantial sum to replace the *face* lost was also required.

Considering Compensation

A word about compensation levels. For the employee who has not worked for an employer in a developing country, the decision to do so will be a profound career experience. It is unlikely that the position will be occupied by the same person for more than a few years. The usual basis for issuance of employee work permits by immigration authorities is that the employee will provide some capability that local talent does not have. Also, he or she will be expected to *transfer* the *technology* that underlies the employee's special capability to native employees. As soon as this transfer is accomplished (in theory at least), the employee will be required to leave. The intervening years may be few or many, but it is unlikely to be a lifetime job. Paradoxically, the more the employee cooperates in training native employees, the more likely that his or her work permit will be extended. If the employee's image evolves into that of a guru, then he or she may, indeed, be there forever.

Keeping up with technological changes will be somewhat more difficult, simply because the employee will be out of the mainstream of his or her profession; employees are typically remote from seminars, continuing education, similar professional activities, and the ever important "network" system. The employee's expertise and value in the marketplace back home may not be equal to contemporaries after several years overseas. As a result, finding a challenging job opportunity back home at the end of the overseas contract may be difficult.

Therefore, the experience may prove to be a discontinuity in one's career and should be given careful consideration when determining compensation. The employee will not likely receive retirement benefits or a pension as a result of the employment and, in some cases (depending on country of origin), the employee may stand to lose some or all home country social benefits. Therefore, compensation negotiations should include allowances for these factors. While pricing oneself out of the market should be avoided, the employee should not consider accepting a job with an employer in a developing country at the same pay level as he or she would with a multinational firm where there is at least the possibility of a long-term commitment. There will be more about compensation in the conditions of employment.

Negotiating Ability Indicates a Level of Competence

Employers in all countries want their employees to look out for the company's interest, to obtain the highest profit, to reduce costs through greater efficiency, and to aspire to similar goals. This is understandable and should be accepted by any employee, whether expatriate or native.

If the employee is not able to sell himself or herself to negotiate the best *realistic* terms, then it is unlikely that these skills will suddenly be acquired when negotiating on behalf of the employer. Fair and equitable employment terms achieved through one-on-one negotiations should build mutual respect and will tell the employer a lot about the employee, and vice versa.

Dispelling Misinformation about Expatriate Compensation

Expatriates receive a higher income than native employees. This is because the expatriate employee has some ability that the employer needs and is willing to pay for. While this is a pure business decision, it may be difficult for some native employees to accept, since the inference is that the expatriate employee is more valuable than his or her native counterparts. While this may be correct in a business sense, it is often taken in a personal way.

When employees (expatriate or native) find themselves in such a situation, the tendency is to rationalize an explanation, usually one that avoids the real reason. If left unchecked such rationalizations and the misinformation that results tend to grow, building tension in the organization. Situations such as described serve no benefit for either the employer or the employee. If left unchecked the employee may find it difficult to perform to the best of his or her ability (or at all) because of a lack of cooperation from key native employees. This is a problem that the employer needs to be aware of and correct immediately when detected.

The employee, who is expected to perform to the best of his or her ability, cannot be expected to accept or carry feelings of guilt or responsibility for prior periods of colonialism or the inequities that may exist between the wealthy and poor in these countries. The employee is not there to either justify or deny past injustices nor to meddle in the political or social structure of the country, but simply to do his or her job as best as possible for the benefit of the employer. However, this does not mean that the employee (and/or family) shouldn't participate in volunteer work for the needy, local clinics, and other similar activities. Such aid is always welcome.

Paying the Employee to Avoid Internal Conflict

Where possible, the employee should be paid out of an account and by persons remote from the employer's staff that process the native payroll. Even when employee compensation is handled by the chief finance officer of the company, there is no guarantee that the conditions of employment will remain confidential. If these conditions are *not* kept confidential, indigenous staff soon know the terms of the employment agreement, including what the employee is being paid. No matter how objective these persons, a sense of resentment may develop that could result in a lack of cooperation with the employee. Paradoxically, it's the employer who may lose the most, since the employee will not be able to achieve as much as he or she otherwise could have with the full cooperation of the indigenous staff. The employee can also help prevent or reduce resentment by not flaunting his or her relatively greater wealth and by living in a reasonably conservative lifestyle.

The Work Schedule

Some special jobs in remote places, such as often found in the oil industry, require a twelve hour on/twelve hour off/work schedule. Such a schedule is not common in most other industries. In any case, the employer should be reasonably specific about the normal work schedule and time off. While it is recognized that maximum effort may be necessary for short periods (as would be expected in a crisis), no one can work effectively seven days per week, fourteen hours (or more) per day, for weeks (or months) at a time. Productivity diminishes rapidly after the first week of such a schedule. On the other hand, if working long hours for weeks is *normal* in a company (or for an individual), then it is likely that:

- There is insufficient planning.
- There is lack of delegation.
- Goals are too ambitious for the quantity of resources available.
- The people involved do not have the organizational or technical skills needed to complete assignments during normal hours.
- The organizational processes are not in place.

It's important for the employer and employee to discuss the work schedule so that the employee will have a full understanding of what is expected. It's better for one or both parties to break off negotiations if their philosophies concerning work hours (and habits) do not coincide. The employee simply won't meet the employer's expectations.

For example, it is not unusual to find executives in developing countries out late at night (practically every night) with social and business commitments. As a result, they may not arrive at the office until 10:00 A.M. or 11:00 A.M. (or later) the next day. The Executive then starts his work day, which runs until 8:00 P.M. or 9:00 P.M. (or later). During the executive's work day, key staff members are expected to be available. The staff, on the other hand, are generally in the office by 7:30 A.M. to 8:00 A.M. which means the staff are putting in very long work days. This creates a paradox because it is the rare company in developing countries where even routine decisions are made below the chief executive level. As a result, the morning hours are not always as productive for the staff as they could be.

2

The Conditions of Employment

1. Duration of Employment

The months shown in paragraph 8 of the employment agreement letter are calendar months. It is agreed that this is the time in which the employee will be available for normal work routine. Any vacation or short leave that may accrue shall be in addition to the months shown.

What the employer is interested in, generally, is the time that the employee's expertise will be needed for the employer to achieve his goals. Therefore, the time that the employee will be available each day at the office or job site throughout the agreement period is what's important. For example, if the employer has made a study and estimated, with reasonable accuracy, that it will take two years of *effort* to put a Management Information System (MIS) into operation, then that is the time the employee will have to be at the office. All other activities, such as vacations, would be additional. However, some employers may prefer a fixed term, such as on construction projects, in which case the wording must be modified.

2. Family Status

This agreement includes family status for the covered dependents of employee as listed in paragraph 5 of the employment agreement letter.

Obviously, this only applies to an employee who has a family. For the single or the divorced individual who wishes to have family members visit at certain times of the year, the wording would have to be modified.

3. Transportation from and Return to Point of Origin

Employer agrees to furnish prepaid, round-trip (also known as return airfare), business-class air transportation, at the full-fare rate, for employee and covered dependents, from employee's point of origin to employee's permanent residence place, shown in paragraphs 6 and 9 respectively of the employment agreement letter, and for employee's and covered dependents' return to employee's point of origin, at the completion or termination of this agreement, whichever comes first. Employee and covered dependents shall, under all circumstances, have the right to select the air carrier providing transportation services.

The reason that the *full-fare* rate should be specified is that tickets obtained on any other basis are normally limited to use on the issuing airline or at a specific time. Therefore, if the specified airline has to cancel or delay the intended flight, the passenger with other than a full-fare ticket will not be able to switch to a different carrier. This is obviously undesirable when one is concerned with sticking to a schedule, which is always the case in overseas work.

4. Schedule of Payments to Employee

Employee shall be paid, on the last, or nearest, working day at the end of each month, the monthly base salary shown in paragraph 3 of the employment agreement letter. Bonuses shall be paid (monthly or at the end of each twelve (12) months work period, select as appropriate) or earlier at employer's sole discretion (such as: hardship leave, religious holidays, etc.). The amounts shown for monthly base salary and bonuses are the net amount(s) to be paid to employee after all deductions for personal income and other taxes, social benefits and similar deductions (except as may be due to the tax authority in employee's country of origin which shall be the sole responsibility of employee). Payment of all compensation due employee shall be to the bank account or cash disbursement shown in attachment II. Any delays in the receipt of funds due employee shall bear interest at the rate of two (2) percent per month or proration thereof.

Needless to say, this is an important paragraph. The first sentence concerns on what day of the month the employee can expect to receive his pay, and it is straightforward. Note that the amounts shown in the employment agreement letter are *net* pay, in other words the amount the employee is to receive each month (and when bonuses become due) after all deductions. This is a sure way to avoid one of the principal disagreements that often arise. Calculating deductions is best left to the employer's staff and does not need to involve the employee.

The second concerns bonuses. Some judgment will be required by both the employer and employee in determining when bonuses will be paid. This is essentially a risk-analysis process that should include consideration of the employer's type of business and history of failures in that type of enterprise and other similar factors. If the risk is high, but the employer doesn't want to pay a bonus directly to the employee monthly, then an alternate solution is for an interest-bearing account to be set up in the name of the employee into which the employer deposits the monthly bonus amount. The account is structured in such a way that the employee receives the interest each month but cannot withdraw the amounts deposited until a certain date or at the end of each year (or at termination), at which time the employee withdraws the full amount. The employer pays any taxes that may come due as a result of the bonus and interest paid. The employee should not, under most conditions, be required to place his income at risk. One condition that would alter this is if the employee is brought in as one of the owners of the company.

The third sentence is also straightforward and should need no explanation. The fourth concerns where the funds due the employee are to be deposited. This is more fully described in attachment II.

The last sentence, concerning interest on overdue salary and bonus amounts, may seem onerous to the employer. There are many reasons why an employer in either developed or developing countries may be late making the payroll. However, the risk is somewhat higher in developing countries, not necessarily due to any intent on the part of the employer, but because the employer may not be able to collect money owed him as readily or in time to pay his employees when due. On the other hand, if the employer feels his business is and will remain financially sound, then there should be no objection to this language being in the agreement, since no such interest payment will ever be made. The principle presented here is that employees should not be put in a position of essentially (and unwillingly) *financing* their employer's business unless, as mentioned above, the employee is one of the owners of the company. This principle is fundamental in either developed or developing countries.

5. *Employee's Personal Income Taxes*

Employer is solely responsible for the prompt payment of any personal income tax liability of employee that may become payable under the laws of and in any country where employer may require employee to work or travel and which results from compensation and/or any benefits employee receives under the terms of the agreement. Employer shall be solely responsible for the accuracy of all tax information related to compensation and benefits provided to or for employee under the terms of the agreement and shall pay all interest or fines, if any, that may come due as a result of incorrect information supplied to tax authorities. Employer shall provide free tax consultation to the employee through an internationally recognized firm such as (for example only) Arthur Anderson or KPMG. Employee is solely responsible for complying with the tax laws of employee's country of origin. Employer agrees to furnish employee, concurrent with each monthly and bonus amount paid, a statement of accounts, on employer's company letterhead, signed by the chief financial officer of employer's company, showing employee's gross and net income earned, amount of income, social benefit, and other taxes and benefits withheld for the current month and the total of these same amounts for the calendar year to date. Failure to provide this information shall be considered a material breach of the agreement.

Unless the employee is a tax specialist, he or she will find it impossible to navigate through the tax laws of developing countries (in some cases even his or her own country). In some developing countries such laws are often administered on a negotiable basis. For example, a company may pay no taxes all year and at the end of the year bargain with the authorities on the amount to be paid. As part of the negotiating process, the information submitted to the tax authorities may not be totally accurate for either native or expatriate employees. Such practices are common in many such countries and make predictable (and accurate) tax planning for the employee impossible. In any case, there is an *unknown* involved that cannot realistically be absorbed by the employee. Therefore, the employment agreement should be clear that any taxes whatsoever that become due, in any country that the employer requires the employee to work, will be for the account of the employer. This should include payment of *taxes on taxes* because if the employer pays the taxes due, such payment will likely be looked upon as additional income for the employee.

For some employees the taxes paid by the employer are also treated as regular income when submitting home country tax forms.

Therefore, some careful planning should be done, although it may be impossible to estimate exact exposure where the employee is moving from country to country several times a year such as on construction projects.

Obtaining a statement of taxes withheld and paid by the employer can be difficult for the previous reasons. The employer will often not be able to provide a formal document from his country's tax authorities stating the proportion allocated to the employee's income and benefits where a *lump sum* settlement has been negotiated with the authority. For most employees this will not be a problem, since they do not have to pay home country taxes at all when working overseas. For the remaining minority, getting such a statement is vital because the information is needed to complete annual home country tax returns. As mentioned previously, the employee should seek professional accounting advice prior to signing the employment agreement.

One last comment about taxes. It should be noted that those employees who have to pay home country taxes on their foreign income are at a distinct commercial disadvantage. For example, a citizen of the United Kingdom who makes $10,000 per month in another country will likely get to keep all of it, although a U.S. citizen is subject to taxes on all income over a specified amount. This puts the U.S. citizen in a position of possibly having to accept an overall lesser annual take-home pay than his U.K. counterpart, even though they do the same work. Therefore, the employer, knowing this, tries to negotiate the U.K. citizen down to the approximate take-home pay level of his U.S. counterpart, or offers a lower living allowance, etc., to offset the difference. Both the U.K. and U.S. employees lose as a result. Because of the difficulties of the more complicated situation of the U.S. citizen (he or she requires more paperwork), some foreign employers may prefer not to hire U.S. citizens.

6. Retirement and Other Social Benefits

Employer shall not withhold or pay any unemployment, social benefit or similar taxes to employee's country of origin. Employee will receive no pension or retirement benefits under the agreement except as may be required by the laws in the country, or countries, in which employee is required to work by the employer.

Multinational companies usually include what is termed a *hypothetical* tax clause in employment agreements. In essence, this says that the employee's base pay (and other allowances) will not be taxed any greater amount than they would in the employee's home country. If they are, then the employer pays (or is responsible) for the additional amount. As of this writing, there is no procedure in place for a developing country employer, with no established business in the employee's home country, to comply with the tax regulations of the employee's home country. Even some multinational companies, when transferring an employee overseas, "terminate" the employee from his or her home country job and "employ" the employee in a wholly-owned subsidiary outside their principal domicile (usually in a country considered a tax haven), to avoid the administrative burden of accounting for and paying taxes to the tax authorities in the employee's home country. The employee will have to study his or her own situation carefully and make such contributions or such other necessary arrangements according to the laws of his or her home country.

7. Visas, Work Permits, and Similar Documents

Employer shall be responsible for all costs associated with the processing of visas, work permits, exit visas, payment of airport tax, fiscal tax, and any other taxes, fees, permits, clearances or similar that may be required for employee's and covered dependents' residence in, and departure from, the employer assigned permanent residence place, or any other country to which employee is required to travel for the business purposes of employer, or as otherwise provided for in the agreement. Employer agrees to provide employee and covered dependents with current exit visas at all times so as to provide immediate departure from the permanent residence place for medical treatment or for any other reason at the sole discretion of employee or covered dependents. Exit visas (or permits) shall be reprocessed prior to expiration dates in order to fulfill this requirement. Failure to provide current exit visas (or permits) at all times shall be considered a material breach of the agreement.

The employee should not contact or try to obtain information directly from the foreign embassy of the country where he or she plans to be employed, without first getting instructions from the prospective employer. There may be specific procedures or protocol to be followed which, if not carried out precisely, could delay or prevent the employee's departure to the employer's country. In the best of situations, processing of work permits can take six months or more. The employer may need the employee before that. If the employee has contacted the employer's embassy or consulate prematurely, it may become difficult to impossible for the employer to take the necessary steps to shorten the six-month time required before the employee can enter and work in the country.

If the employer does need the employee in less than the usual processing time, then he will resolve this with the authorities in his home country and arrange for the employee to work *temporarily* on a business visa or some similar document or *facility* as it is often called. In this case, the work permit will likely be processed in country. When it is finally approved and ready for issue, the employee will typically be required to fly to a nearby country where he or she will be met by the employer's agent. The agent will take the employee's passport to the embassy of the country of intended employment and have the necessary papers processed and the employee's passport stamped appropriately. This typically takes one to two days. The employee's dependents will usually have to do the same.

The employer must furnish complete instructions concerning the personal papers that will be required to process visas, work permits, and so forth for the employee and the employee's dependents. The employee should not be surprised if the information needed goes far beyond what would normally be readily available. In some countries, the documents may have to be originals. If copies are the only ones available, then proof that the documents are *true copies* will likely be required. There is no typical list of what may be needed, but the following list is at least a beginning that anyone wishing to work overseas should have as a start:

- Current passports with expiration dates greater than the intended stay
- Birth certificates, originals preferred, certified copies may be acceptable
- Baptismal certificates, originals preferred
- Marriage license
- Divorce papers, if applicable
- Military discharge papers, other certificates of training and advancement
- High school and university diplomas
- Certificates of achievement for any additional training

- Any awards that may have been received that are applicable to the type of work contemplated
- Professional licenses or certificates
- Immunization record on the international form
- International driver's license
- Current, detailed resume for the person seeking the work permit
- Spare passport photos

In addition to finding all of the right papers, it is sometimes required that the employee be able to prove where he or she was on a certain date or dates. This typically has to do with the country's desire to keep foreigners out who may have, in some way, supported the losing side in a recent political crisis.

One of the most sensitive matters that the employee may encounter is the disregard for confidentiality often displayed by the native employees who process work permits. As mentioned, the information required by the authorities borders on what is needed for a high-priority security clearance in the employee's home country. Yet, such files are not always kept in secure storage and are often available to any employee of the company who happens to be curious about another employee's background or that of any member of his or her family. Such casual treatment of personal and private information is often taken by the employee as rude (if not shocking).

8. *Temporary Accommodations When Arriving and Departing*

All costs of temporary accommodations, food, laundry, dry cleaning, telephone, facsimile, and telex required by employee and employee's covered dependents, while employee is seeking a permanent residence at the permanent residence place or, as may be required during packing in preparation for employee's and employee's covered dependents permanent return to employee's point of origin, will be prearranged and paid for by employer. Such temporary accommodations will be in a first class hotel (Four Star), or equivalent private guest house (employee and dependents only in residence), or better. Employer will provide the services of a professional real estate company to aid employee in locating a permanent residence.

This is self-explanatory, but it requires a few comments. Problems usually occur because the employee and dependents spend more time each day while in temporary accommodations than the employer had anticipated. Even the term *reasonable costs* may have a different meaning to each party. So, there needs to be an understanding of what is meant by "All costs of temporary accommodations, food, laundry, dry cleaning, telephone, facsimile, and telex. . . ."

For example, the employer probably does not intend that the employee and dependents be given the presidential suite as temporary accommodations or that they consistently eat in the most expensive restaurant in the hotel. What is more likely expected is a daily cost consistent with the quality of accommodations and services normally acceptable to the employer for his other employees in a similar position and status while on business trips, plus the cost of providing the employee's dependents similar facilities and services.

At the same time, the accommodations need to be large enough that the employee and dependents can achieve some individual privacy, especially if they are to be in this facility for an extended period. There should also be sufficient drawers and closets to put away personal belongings so that it is not necessary "to live out of one's suitcase" or hang clothing from hooks on the wall. This includes space to put away suitcases as well, or the facility to store these in the hotel.

Telephone calls, especially international calls, are typically very expensive when initiated through the hotel switchboard, even where the hotel has a direct dial facility, sometimes even when the calls are charged to the other end. Not too many years ago, I talked to my wife from a certain Southeast Asian country for 10 minutes and the cost was over $200! It pays to check rates and the extra charges tacked on beforehand to prevent (expensive) surprises.

One way to reduce this cost is to use a home country telephone credit card. U.S. citizens who maintain a telephone in the U.S. while on overseas assignment can obtain a credit card from a telephone service company. Other countries have equivalent services. These cards can be used from within practically all developed countries and many developing countries by dialing a special access number. Obviously, if calls are made through this facility, then the cost will have to be recovered through an expense account; that is, if the call is a legitimate business expense.

There is a method of reducing the cost of an international call from a hotel. The procedure has to be established beforehand with the person or persons normally called. A person-to-person call is placed, collect, to the name of a relative who, it is known beforehand, will not be there. When the operator replies that the person is not there the call is canceled. This is a signal for the "real" person being called to place the call from his or her location, at a much reduced rate.

A particular subject that should be addressed is the use and cost of alcoholic beverages. Due to religious beliefs, the employer may frown on beer and other alcoholic beverages showing up on the hotel bill. Bar bills may not be allowed unless they are for business entertainment purposes. Sometimes even then they are not allowed. More about this in article 23, "Business Expenses."

One of the most important items that the employee should investigate before accepting a job overseas (especially in a developing country) is the availability of expert medical care. The name or names and telephone numbers of medical practitioners recommended by the employer or other employees who have lived in the area should be obtained. If at all possible, this must be done before arriving in the country. The reason is that the probability of getting ill is more likely just after getting off the plane than at most other times, especially for young dependents.

9. Employee's Permanent Residence

Employer agrees to furnish an air-conditioned, fully-furnished residence or accommodations (or partially furnished at employee's option) for employee and covered dependents of a style and size, and in a location commensurate to employee's position but in no case of less standard than that provided for the employer's client's staff of equivalent position or title, or the quality specified in attachment 4 to the agreement. Accommodations shall include employer paid utilities, telephone, garbage collection, taxes (if any), and security guard services.

Locating and choosing employee housing is often a major problem in many developing countries. It is not unusual to find quarters of much better or much less quality than the employee is used to. The neighborhoods will probably fit this same pattern. In small, out of the way locations there may be limited choice, while in large metropolitan areas the number of available houses to choose from may be overwhelming. In some major cities, it is not unusual to visit as many as 80 houses in an attempt to find the "right" one. The employee should be prepared and organized for this possibility. He or she should have a notebook, camera, portable tape recorder (or camcorder), and the best map of the area when looking. These items should be kept in a separate bag or briefcase ready to go when a new prospect is visited.

When selecting a house, it should be remembered that a lot more time will be spent inside the house than in the employee's country of origin. For example, a lovely house may be found behind a 14-foot high security wall but located in a neighborhood where it would be impractical for the children to play on the street. Therefore, the house needs to have enough inside space and grounds so that each person in residence can have a reasonable level of privacy.

Many developing countries tend to be extremely noisy, sometimes at all hours of the day and night. An employee sensitive to noise should visit prospective houses at various times to ensure that the noise level will be tolerable. Also, it could be important to know about public or religious gatherings that may take place periodically in the neighborhood. Some of these can go on for days.

10. Repairs to Employee's Residence

Should the employee's residence need repair, employer agrees to immediately undertake and pay for said repairs notwithstanding the responsibility of the property owner in any contract between the employer and the property owner. Should the repairs not be completed immediately then employee shall have the option of moving into temporary accommodations as described in paragraph 8 above at employer's expense until repairs have been completed. Employer reserves the right to negotiate the final agreement with the owner of the property chosen by employee. Refer to attachment 4 which outlines the minimum standard of housing that will be provided for employee.

This subject can be one of the most annoying for the employee, and especially the spouse, who has to look after the household each day. Neither the employee nor spouse is in a good position to organize household repairs, especially just after arrival. As a matter of fact, the employee has not likely been hired by the employer to spend time looking after such matters.

As mentioned in the second sentence, there needs to be provision for the family moving into temporary accommodations if the repairs are not made immediately. Examples might be a leaking roof, flooding, loss of one or more utilities for a sustained period, contaminated water, dangerous structural damage caused by termites, earthquake, or storm, and similar circumstances.

How do you define *immediately* as used in the first sentence? Obviously, this depends upon the severity of damage or importance of the repair needed. The employee should receive a *verbal* response immediately in all cases, a *physical* response within an hour for serious items, and within 24 hours for minor ones.

The following are some examples of repairs that need *immediate* response:

- A leaking roof that is soaking furniture and carpets. A repair team should be dispatched within the hour to at least install plastic sheeting over the part of the roof that is leaking to prevent further damage. A roofing contractor should arrive immediately after the rain has stopped (in daylight, of course) and make permanent repairs. The temporary plastic cover should not become the permanent repair by default.

- An air-conditioner failure may be more than just a comfort problem if, for example, screens are missing or damaged, or if there are no screens on the windows at all and opening the windows will let in snakes, rats, or malaria-carrying mosquitoes.

- Damaged or broken locks on doors and windows.

- Leaking LPG or natural gas.

- An electrical shock while in the shower or swimming pool.

- Fire damage.

The following are some typical minor items:

- An electrical receptacle that has burned out or stopped working, with no further damage. However, this could be critical if the refrigerator is connected to this receptacle and there is no alternate.

- A large number of light bulbs burning out each week for no apparent reason (probably voltage surge).

- Sticking doors.

- Leaking faucet.

At the same time, the employee should not expect the employer to send out a repair crew for changing light bulbs, electrical fuses, and similar.

11. Security Guard Service

Employer will provide uniformed security guard service specifically for and at the residence of employee. Security guard service will be furnished on a 24 hour per day basis. No less than two (2) guards will be employed each day, one (1) for daytime and one (1) for night time service (or more, as appropriate). Employer shall obtain security guards from a professional security service which is recognized and licensed by the local police. Employee shall have the right to participate in the selection of and have replaced any or all security guard(s) assigned to the protection of employee's residence at employee's sole discretion.

The following paragraphs will deal with security matters around the employee's residence. Some people simply do not like to discuss home or personal security as it conjures up unpleasant visions. This is unfortunate since such persons will not be mentally prepared should an incident arise. When not prepared the usual result is panic and mistakes, sometimes at the expense of other family members. This book would not be complete without some comments about security. This information is not intended to cause concern but present realistic considerations that should be addressed. One does not have to be any more afraid in most developing countries than in any developed country, and in some cases a lot less. In both worlds, being observant and prepared goes a long way towards prevention. No criminal is going to break into facilities with good security provisions when there are less secure places from which to choose. Therefore, think of the following as you would information concerning winter driving hazards and how they can be avoided.

Security guards are a necessity in most developing countries. Depending on the particular circumstances, such as location of the house, local crime rate, and the political situation, guards may be needed both day and night, perhaps more than one guard on each shift if the property is large. To obtain personal effects insurance, the employee will likely have to verify the existence of security guards on duty 24 hours per day at the residence. Make a special note to verify this with the insurance company.

Security services have to be chosen carefully just as in any other part of the world. The best guards will probably be professional military or police, either retired or "moonlighting." The employee should not consider using the gardener, house boy, or some similar person for this task unless living inside a high-security compound. Even then, the employee should think long and hard about this choice.

There are definite reasons for choosing professionals. The typical nonprofessional will sleep at night unless the employee makes a habit of getting up at all hours to check. This, of course, isn't realistic if the employee has to be well rested each morning. Typically, nonprofessionals don't want trouble with intruders, especially the possibility of getting injured, and will tend to look the other way when it is evident that a confrontation is about to occur. If the nonprofessional does confront an intruder and calls for help, the police may not respond enthusiastically because he isn't part of the "professional" fraternity.

When a crime is committed, the police may take the attitude that the crime would *not* have occurred if security had been provided by professionals; therefore, the police do little to solve the case. When the nonprofessional does sneak off to sleep (typically under a car in the garage), he will often leave garage door and house keys in obvious view in hopes that the benevolence of the gesture will prevent any aggression being directed his way. No matter how great the salary the employee may receive, it won't be enough if he or she does not feel personally secure.

Obviously, this possibility is not uncommon to developed countries. The difference is that in developing countries the employee is noticeable, is a relatively easy target, and will generally have more valuable personal property. Also, employees are seldom allowed to own or keep firearms, which means there is little danger to anyone who wishes to enter the premises, especially if professional security guards are not present. Besides, if the employee isn't trained in the use of firearms, it can be more of a liability than help in a confrontation.

In many countries there are laws that actually defend the person who assaults or robs (even murders) an employee. The principle is that if the employee wasn't there, then the confrontation couldn't have taken place. In such countries the employee may be (automatically) judged to be the one wrong and asked to leave the country, while the criminal (by any other standards) may be punished minimally or even set free.

Where it is legal, security guards should be armed with a handgun kept loaded at all times. This needs to be at least .38 caliber or larger. A smaller caliber weapon does not have reliable "stopping" power. It is not unusual (if lucky enough to hire military personnel) that they will be allowed by their commanding officer to carry their service weapon while performing off-duty security services. Very often this weapon will be an M-16, AK-47, or similar firearm. Needless to say, if a confrontation occurs, and the guards are carrying such firearms, it's important to stay out of the line of fire.

The employee should pack several professional-quality flashlights in his or her sea shipment. The best are the black-anodized aluminum type typically used by police units in the United States and available through most sporting goods stores. The five-cell size is the best. These should be equipped with the so-called "Krypton" bulbs. Several extra bulbs should be purchased for each flashlight. These special bulbs give off a brilliant light. A flashlight is needed for each security guard, one for each bedroom, and at least one spare. One manufacturer also makes a small miniature of the big ones that fits neatly into pocket or purse.

All of the employee's household staff should be registered with the local police or similar authority applicable to the particular country. A list of each staff member's local and permanent home address, telephone number (rare for staff), next of kin, and references is also necessary. Also, make photos to go with these records. The employee should keep one copy at home, give one to the authorities, and put one in a safe deposit box or similar secure place.

Knowing that the employee and the employer take security seriously and that suspects can be easily identified and traced will reduce the probability of household staff being involved. The employee should be firm about relatives and guests of household staff who come to visit, especially entering the house. The number of such visits should be limited and a specific place set aside (other than inside the expatriate's residence) where meetings will take place.

The employee should not discard personal letters, bank statements, packing boxes in which electronic equipment or similar were packed in the garbage. Instead, shred and burn or dispose of these off the premises. Clues as to what is in a house are often dug out of the trash by persons working with criminals.

Before admitting any workmen such as plumbers, electricians, pest control personnel, and so forth, the employee should verify that they are registered with their employer, carry identification, and have a work order signed by their employer authorizing the work. The names of all workmen should be listed on the work order. A copy of this should be retained by the employee. If the employee can't personally stay home while the work is being done, the most trusted member of the household staff should be there. This will usually be the cook, who is typically considered the senior person. Note that the pest control man normally has access to every room (nook and cranny) and will know the entire house layout as well as where all valuables are likely to be kept.

If the employee's home has been selected for a robbery, entry may be attempted during a rain storm. The sound of the rain tends to conceal noise, and footprints are soon lost in the mud. Identification through fingerprinting is not yet widespread in many developing countries, and it is not considered a major hazard by intruders. It is a good practice to lock all doors, even to rooms not in use, because this will slow an intruder down, although it may not stop him. Children are often instructed not to leave their bedrooms no matter what they hear or how scared they may get unless given a specific verbal signal from a parent (with the exception of a fire).

At least one dog should be obtained as a security aid. Some employees have one dog that stays in the children's bedroom area at night and one in the parents' bedroom. The dog(s) should be trained and disciplined and not allowed to run around the neighborhood or become friendly with strangers. (Also, in some countries dogs are still a delicacy.)

One final comment about security. Thoroughly check the roof for loose tiles, vent screens, etc. because burglars can gain access to these areas from adjacent structures and trees. Remove trees or branches that may provide access to the roof. Add barbed wire or metal grills in other locations. Check roof tiles and attic vents to be sure they can't easily be pried loose. Where the roof has a large overhang, insure that the ceiling or soffit material under the overhang is secure.

In closing this commentary, I want to, again, emphasize that attention to security matters should be of no more concern than daily hazards one might encounter in any country. Being prepared and observant is the best formula for peace of mind.

12. Dependent Schooling

Employer agrees to provide school bond (where applicable), tuition, school bus (air-conditioned, if appropriate and available), and any other fees at an international school accredited in employee's country of origin and nearest to the permanent residence place for each dependent child, or an equivalent amount should employee elect to enroll dependent children in other insti-

tutions either locally or abroad. Employer shall only furnish education expenses for undergraduate dependent children in kindergarten through twelfth grade of the American system high school, or equivalent European plan, at employee's option and, for dependents up to and including age twenty-five (25). The costs of tuition, books and fees (but not accommodations, food and other, miscellaneous personal expenses) up to US $ _____ per year will be provided for covered dependents enrolled in a full-time university course in an accredited university.

Schools vary so greatly in quality and location that the employee with school age children is pretty much on his or her own in deciding the best solution for any particular set of circumstances. The school authorities in most developed nations can provide some information on overseas schools, although this is sometimes grossly inaccurate. The best source of information is from parents and children who have experience in the particular country. In my experience, all overseas schools have provided an excellent education for our children.

13. Employee's and Covered Dependents' Personal Effects

Employer shall provide all costs of packing, storage, and transport of employee's and covered dependents' personal effects, from employee's point of origin to employee's permanent residence at the permanent residence place. Such costs shall include but are not limited to: the cost of personal effects valuation and inventory preparation, packaging, transport, replacement cost insurance coverage, controlled climate (e.g., temperature and humidity) storage at point of origin of all personal effects not shipped to employee's permanent residence place, storage in-transit in climate controlled facilities (where storage in-transit is required), customs formalities and duties, delivery and unpacking, and removal from the residence of packing materials. Employee's sea shipment is limited to an amount equivalent to one (1) forty (40) foot container. Employee and covered dependents are allowed a maximum of 20 kilograms, or one (1) extra suitcase per person excess baggage while in transit. Employee is allowed one (1) air freight shipment of a maximum of 1,000 kilograms packaged weight for unaccompanied baggage. All of the provisions of this article 13 shall also apply to employee's and covered dependents' return to point of origin at completion or termination of this agreement, but not in case of employee's annual vacation with intent to return to the same permanent residence place to complete this agreement or in case this agreement should be extended in which case these same amounts shall apply at the end of the extended period. Employee shall have the right to select the packers and shippers of employee's personal effects. Where shipping by ocean freight is required, the container shall be carried in a dry hold, below main deck.

No packing or shipping should commence until the employee has made a complete inventory. This should include the name of each item, number of similar items, manufacturer, where purchased, date purchased, original cost, current replacement cost (not *present cash value* which includes allowance for depreciation), where it is located or to be located (i.e., left at home, placed in storage, or shipped) and serial and model numbers (as appropriate). Books should also be inventoried in a similar way including the names of author and publisher and date of publication. Antiques and similar valuables should be appraised by a registered professional who should issue a certificate of authenticity and value. The employee is advised to keep the quantity of valuable items transported to the new domicile overseas to a minimum.

If the employee has a personal computer or access to one, compiling such a list is tedious but easily accomplished with any of the popular data base programs. The employee should use a camera (or camcorder) to record as many of the items as possible on film. Do try to segregate according to eventual location. A picture of, for example, a table with all the fine china laid out can provide a good indication of quality to the insurance adjuster in case of a claim.

One copy of the inventory and photos should be sent by registered mail to the insurance underwriter to keep on file. The employee should put one copy in a safe place in his or her home country and make copies for the packers; do this separately for those items being shipped and those being stored.

Items going into a container (usually 40 feet long) should be professionally packed in cardboard boxes first, then into heavy wooden crates called "lift vans." Lift vans are large and are usually built to just slide inside the container. The lift vans should be lined with water-resistant material, just in case rain or sea water does get inside the container. Be sure that the final "as-packed" configuration has about two inches between the bottom of the lift vans and the inside bottom of the container. This will provide at least some capacity for water that may get in to settle and drain. Ask for the more valuable items to be located in the upper part of the lift vans where feasible. Packing loose items in a container should not be accepted.

Lift vans should be made out of one-half inch type CDX (exterior grade) plywood and no less than two by four framing material. The lift vans should be mounted on skids, nailed shut, and banded. Smaller crates should be made from one-quarter inch CDX plywood using framing material appropriate to the size of the crate. The smaller crates go inside lift vans. Lift vans should be painted over the entire outside a specific color for easy identification and stenciled with the employee's name as well as all shipping instructions.

If shipping computers and similar electronic equipment by sea, be sure that a moisture absorbent is inside the plastic outer wrap and that the plastic is well sealed. Do not let the packers throw loose items into their van for packing later at their warehouse, unless the shipment is originating from a location that is too difficult to reach by the truck with the lift vans. If the employee's personal effects must be repacked at the warehouse, arrangements should be made to be there to observe the proceedings and count the pieces.

The employee should have a clear understanding with the packer and shipper that the container and all contents are to be inspected by the employee before closing. The employee should provide the lock that goes on the container. This should be the best industrial-duty lock available that will fit the hasp on the container doors. The employee should keep the keys. Be sure this understanding includes that the container and the lift van(s) and crate(s) inside are not to be opened, under any circumstances, unless the employee is present, at both shipping and receiving points.

The shipper should be questioned carefully about the sea route that the container will take. Where possible, have the shipper arrange booking on a ship that will carry the container all the way to the final destination with the least amount of handling of the container. Try to eliminate transshipment of the container at some remote foreign port. The more a container is handled, the greater the possibility of damage. Also, there have been some countries that require all cargo entering their ports to be opened and inspected before forwarding.

The shipping company representative on the receiving end in a developing country may urge the employee not to attend the opening of the container for customs inspection on the basis that the *unoffi-cial* charges will be higher if the employee is there for the customs to intimidate. There is some legitimacy to this. However, it is also not unusual that the customs personnel find items they feel should be *appropriated* and which end up missing when the owner isn't present. The shipper isn't going to tell what really happened because he has to deal with the local customs daily and could have serious difficulties in the future if he talks too much or causes trouble.

How to handle such situations will depend a lot on the country, the circumstances of the moment, and the employer's status with local authorities. The employer is in the best position to control or eliminate such problems. The bottom line is that the employment agreement has to state clearly that the employer will pay for *all* costs including those that are *unofficial*. It should be noted that items typically "missing" from the personal effects shipment are those same items that are not found in the local country and are usually difficult to import. Therefore, the employee may have to wait a long time (typically months) before a replacement arrives, if it ever does.

On the other hand, some items may not be replaceable because they can only be imported with the employee's original personal effects consignment. In other words, only *one* such item per shipment may be allowed. The technicality that the item turned up missing only after the container was opened in the receiving country will probably have no effect on the officials. In fact, it could possibly have a negative one because they are, in so many words, being accused of letting the item disappear while in their custody. It is much easier for the officials to rationalize that the employee and packers on the shipping end made an error in the inventory.

Pets can pose special problems when imported into some developing nations. The fact that the employee would air freight a dog, cat, or other pet to some remote spot indicates that there is an emotional attachment. Even though the particular country may not have regulations prohibiting the importation, "difficulties" can be created by those who wish to take advantage of the situation. To resolve these "difficulties" might mean a substantial outlay of cash, often an amount slightly less than the cost of return airfreight to point of origin.

In at least one country, there is an import duty on dogs that is based on the age of the animal. In other words, the older the dog, the higher the duty. In 1987 the duty was the equivalent of $45 for each 3 months of age. So, a family pet age 10 would require a payment of $1,800 in duty alone.

14. Insurance Coverage for Employee's Personal Effects

Employer shall provide insurance, through an internationally recognized company acceptable to employee, which shall pay for the replacement cost of any personal effects of employee or covered dependents as a result of loss resulting from theft or abandonment due to social unrest, riots, military action, declared or undeclared war or similar situations. The employee shall be the named insured. Proof of coverage shall be handed over to the employee concurrent with the signing of the agreement.

While the wording in this paragraph states that the employer is to provide this insurance, the employee will likely have to find an appropriate insurer, make all arrangements, and then arrange with the employer to make the necessary payment. This insurance should cover the *replacement cost* (not current market value) of the employee's personal effects. Coverage should also include loss due to any type of social unrest, civil disturbance, or any other occurrence that could require the employee to abandon personal effects in the country. This insurance should at least be "arranged," if not "in place," prior to shipment of personal effects from the employee's country of origin.

It should be noted that reliable insurance companies can often be found in developing countries that are either directly or indirectly associated with major firms in developed countries. My own experience with them has been excellent.

15. Automobiles

Employer shall provide two (2) automobiles including costs of all fuel, lubricants, tires, periodic tuneups, and other maintenance items, insurance and drivers (inclusive of all driver overtime) to employee for employee's and covered dependents' use during the term of the agreement. The automobiles may be utilized by employee and covered dependents for personal as well as business needs including personal trips. The vehicles are to be new when handed over to employee and shall be replaced every two (2) years with new vehicles. The make and style of these vehicles shall be commensurate with employee's position but in no case less than Toyota Cressida (as of 1987). Colors are to be selected by employee. Automobiles are to be provided with no less than dark, heat reflective glass all around, radio-cassette multiple speaker system, rubber floor mats over carpets and removable, white, washable seat covers, minimum two (2) sets for each auto.

The second auto is for family use. In some locations, and where the spouse and children are "street smart," have lived in developing countries previously, taxis may be a substitute. In any other circumstance, dependents will need the second automobile for shopping, school activities, and so forth, unless the employee does not require reliable and immediately available transportation throughout the day as part of his or her job. For example, some companies may have pool cars for daily use by key employees.

Be sure that the insurance provided by the employer covers the employee and any other dependent who may occasionally drive these vehicles. The employee should obtain his or her own separate, liability coverage in addition to that provided by the employer since the employee or a dependent could be judged at fault in case of an accident, no matter the "real" circumstances.

I know of one case where an employee, with his family in the car, drove completely off the road and stopped when he saw a large bus coming at high speed around a curve toward him. The road was in poor condition and the bus was traveling at such a high speed that it was skidding. The bus came across the on-coming lane, off on the shoulder, and collided with the side of the employee's auto. The employee's arm was crushed and his son even more seriously injured. No one on the bus was injured. The accident occurred miles from any medical aid. Luckily, there was an Australian nurse at a nearby weekend cottage used by employees. She kept the boy alive while help was sent for. The boy lived and fully recovered after a year of excellent medical care in several countries. The father's shoulder also healed. Incredibly, the local judge who examined the case decided that the fault was with the employee who was ". . . driving recklessly, thereby causing the accident."

An employee should obtain an international drivers license before leaving his or her home country. The same applies to any other family member who will be driving. Having such a license can save a lot of paperwork and time in obtaining a permit to drive in the new place of residence.

In some overseas locations, it will be inadvisable for the employee or family members to drive. This is related to the local laws. In other words, the employee could be judged at fault, on the occurrence of an incident, simply because he was in the country, not unlike the previous example.

An incident could also become serious as crowds gather around the scene of an accident. In some countries any driver who is not from the village in which an incident occurs could be held responsible. There is, in such circumstances, the possibility that the automobile could be attacked, stoned, or turned over. It is because of these possibilities that the native driver, involved in an incident in some developing countries, will often flee the scene. It may be considered better to deal with the police in one's home territory after-the-fact than stop to determine if anyone was hurt or to assess the damage. The employee should be advised of what to expect in the country of employment and proceed accordingly.

Personal drivers are a special topic. Preferably they should be able to read and write and know enough of the employee's native language so that a reasonable level of communications can take place. He should also have some formal training in automotive maintenance beyond simply where to put in the gas. He should know the local shops, road network, where the government offices and employer's clients are (if applicable), as well as clubs, schools, the best native markets, restaurants, and so forth. He should have a lot of what is known as "street sense." He will have to get along with the cook and other household staff as well as the employee and his or her family. Above all, he must be a safe driver.

The employee should prepare a list of requirements and make it clear at an early stage what is expected of each driver. These requirements are best translated into the driver's native tongue, typed out, reviewed, and signed and dated by the driver so that there is no misunderstanding. A copy of this should be given to the company's transportation supervisor (if there is one) so that no conflicting instructions develop.

A driver normally starts early in the morning and works until his employer is finished for the day. The driver's base pay is usually low and overtime is generally appreciated. Duties include keeping the vehicle washed and clean daily, being sure that all services are performed on time, and that gas and oil levels are satisfactory. The driver should be punctual and required to wait at the entrance to buildings in plain view so that it isn't necessary to go looking for him. He should always be ready to assist with packages, baggage, and help passengers in and out of the vehicle. In some countries, he may be quick to help men but hesitate to assist women due to custom. This habit can usually be overcome in time if it can be demonstrated that the driver will not lose "face" by also helping ladies.

The employee should make a point of reviewing all automotive service records and receipts for consumables. It is not uncommon that the driver (or the driver and transportation supervisor) will have an "understanding" in which receipts are obtained for which no service was performed and the money thus derived pocketed. If the driver is required to maintain a daily log showing mileage at beginning and end of the day and services performed, verification is simplified. At the same time, it is unrealistic to expect accountability for every cent as the realities of day-to-day existence for the driver and his family require extra income wherever possible. I don't mention this as an excuse but as a fact of life in many developing countries.

Employers in developing countries are sometimes reluctant to let the company drivers fill the fuel tank completely on the theory that so much cash and fuel being handled in one transaction are a sure invitation to steal. Therefore, it is not uncommon to see fuel gauges on one-quarter to one-half full. The down side is that the driver has to make many more stops, at least some of which will be at the most inopportune time for the employee or dependents. One solution is for the employee to personally oversee the process directly, to pay for fuel and oil out of his or her pocket, and to get reimbursed through an expense account.

It's not hard to imagine that drivers are an important asset to the employee and dependents. If chosen carefully, treated fairly and with respect, they gradually become a part of the employee's "family" and may be difficult to leave behind when it's time for the employee to return to his or her country of origin.

16. Vacations

Employee will receive thirty (30) working days paid vacation for each, and at the end of each, twelve (12) calendar months of employment, except that employer agrees to adjustments to allow employee and covered dependents to schedule vacations during normal school vacation periods where reasonably possible.

Employee expressly agrees that employee's vacation periods can be adjusted by employer should job conditions or work in progress require employee's attendance. Employer shall give employee an additional 2-1/2 days paid vacation for each additional month (or proration thereof) employee is required to remain in attendance due to such job requirements. Employer agrees to give employee sixty days (60) written notice should the employer wish to keep employee in attendance past employee's scheduled start of vacation (or end of agreement) period including the date upon which employee can reschedule such annual vacation. In lieu of vacation, employee may elect to receive, at the time of employee's annual vacation, thirty (30) working days pay plus the cost of full fare round-trip business-class air fare for employee and covered dependents and remain on the job. In this case employee will not be entitled to additional 2-1/2 days paid vacation per month as a result of employee remaining on the job. In case of early termination as provided for in articles 26 and 27, vacation benefits shall be prorated up to the date of termination.

This paragraph is self-explanatory. I will only add that the employee should utilize vacations wherever possible. Money is important but so is one's mental health and relationship with family members.

17. Short Leave

In addition to annual vacations, employee and covered dependents domiciled with employee shall be entitled to take five (5) working days short leave every ninety (90) calender days throughout the term of the agreement at the end of each ninety (90) day period. Short leave shall be taken in the location shown in paragraph 13 of the employment agreement letter or alternate location of equivalent overall cost. Employer agrees to pay for all costs of air transport, accommodations, food, laundry, taxi fares to and from airports only, and any exit/entry/airport taxes, fees or duties during such leave periods. Employee shall pay for all personal expenses while on short leave. Unless otherwise agreed to by the employer in writing, the employee cannot accrue short leave and, except as provided for below, any short leave not taken at the end of each ninety-day period shall be forfeited. Should job requirements prevent employee from taking short leave at the end of any ninety day period as scheduled, employer shall notify employee of the revised schedule for that specific short leave, in writing, at least fourteen (14) days prior to the originally scheduled date. In no case will employer require employee to delay taking scheduled short leave by more than thirty (30) calendar days. A delay in any short leave that is required by employer will not delay or otherwise affect the date of employee's next scheduled short leave. Employee shall be paid twice the employee's base salary amount for each day of delay required by employer (calculated by dividing annual base salary by 365 days and multiplying the resulting amount by the number of days delay and then by 2). In case of early termination as provided for in articles 26 and 27, employee shall be paid for accrued short leave benefits up to the date of termination at employee's base salary rate (calculated by dividing annual base salary by 365 and multiplying the resulting amount by the number of days accrued). All references to vacation as in article 16 above and short leave are in addition to employer granted holidays or official public holidays in the country of the permanent residence place.

An employee working in a developing county will be under more pressure day to day than in his or her country of origin. The same applies to dependents, especially the spouse. These pressures result from differences in culture as well as unplanned events. The unplanned events result from simple misunderstandings to gross mistakes. Some problems can be corrected quickly, while others require weeks to repair. Some have little economic impact, while others can be costly. In any case, the result is ever-increasing frustration because the employee (and dependents) can never seem to prevent them from occurring, no matter how well they plan or how well they train native household or office staff. The tension builds and tempers become short. The following are some examples:

- Even after the weeks of formal training the secretarial staff received in computer systems, a month's worth of accounting analysis was lost when a hard disk failed and it was discovered that the backup disks had been reformatted and used for other purposes, because no one took the time to order new ones.

- The maid has been taking the wife's expensive new suit to the cleaners off and on for the last six months. On the next occasion, she inexplicably throws it in the washing machine with the white towels, on hot, and ruins it.

- Mice gnaw through the back of the closet and eat one of your new $200 pair of shoes, which you intended to wear for the next ten years.

- Your monthly pay has been going to the correct account every month for the year and a half since your arrival. However, accounting *somehow* used the wrong account number when transferring the last pay and your bank back home refused to transfer the funds to the correct account without you first coming to the bank in person to sign some papers. This you can't do for another six months.

- You've had an especially bad five days and look forward to a quiet weekend in the garden reading and relaxing. At 9 P.M. on Friday evening, you hear a crowd gathering in the street in front of your house. Suddenly, there is extremely loud music, right across from your gate. You ask the cook what's going on, and you are told that this is the weekend that people from the local village celebrate some religious festival, and they always use this street as a gathering place. They have used it for years. The celebration will go on day and night throughout the weekend. You decide to check into a local hotel. You try to call ahead but the phone is dead. Having no other choice, you pack the family in the car to drive to the hotel. You're delayed because you can't find the keys; the driver forgot to take them out of his pocket when he went home. Never fear! You find the spare set that you keep for just such an emergency and drive for over an hour and finally reach the hotel. When you arrive, reception tells you that the hotel is sold out for the weekend. You drive back to the house. When you're nearly home, you find the street blocked and a special religious service in progress. You won't be able to get into your gate for another two hours. You can't leave the car on the street because it will likely be stolen if you do.

- You have ten guests coming for Thanksgiving. A month in advance you order a large turkey for the occasion. The driver knows a farmer who raises turkeys, has arranged to pick one up early on Thanksgiving, and assures you that it will be at least 18 pounds. At 7 A.M. on Thanksgiving Day, the driver comes into the living room leading the turkey on a string. It weighs all of seven pounds —with feathers (and other parts). Your guests have hamburgers for Thanksgiving.

- You find out from your grocer that strawberries are grown and frozen 1,600 miles south of the city where you live. They are expensive but can be shipped in with other frozen food. There is a minimum order due to the usual size plastic foam container in which they're packed. Several employee families get together and order one container. Payment has to be in advance. Two weeks later the strawberries arrive, not in the refrigerated truck but in a regular van. They have thawed and spoiled.

These stories are typical. While problems do occur daily in developed countries, they are not likely to be of the nature of those previously described.

The employee and dependents who encounter the fewest problems are those who bring with them the habits of detailed daily planning, alertness, and close observation of events around them at all times. At the same time, this need for constant attention to even the smallest detail to anticipate and prevent problems is a major factor in the build up of tension. To this, add the frustration of problems that continue to occur in spite of the effort to prevent them. The pressure builds and needs to be relieved. This is accomplished through the mechanism of the short leave.

The short leave is not intended to be a week of intense overseas travel. Its purpose is rather to "get away" to a location where the employee and dependents have better control of their environment, thereby reducing the daily input of tension-building events. It is not intended as a way of putting one's "head in the sand," but simply a mechanism for relaxation and revitalization of mental health. As some have said, "to charge your batteries."

18. Transportation during Vacations and Short Leave

Employee and covered dependents will be provided prepaid round-trip (also sometimes called "return airfare"), full-fare business-class air transportation to employee's point of origin (or equivalent air fare at employee's option) for vacation purposes. Should employee not be returning to the permanent residence place (such as vacation or short leave taken at the end or termination of the agreement), then employee and employee's covered dependents shall be returned to employee's point of origin as described in articles 3, 7, 8, 13, and 14, and as otherwise provided for in the agreement.

In addition to the vacations and short leaves called for in articles 16 and 17, all covered dependent children through and including age twenty-five (25) shall be given two (2) round-trip, full-fare business-class airline tickets per year to and from their school or university for vacation purposes where the school

*or schools being attended are not in the city of the permanent
residence place.*

This paragraph should need little explanation. I'll only point out
that the additional round-trip tickets for children who are attending
school at some remote location are for the usual Christmas, spring
breaks, or equivalent.

19. *Medical Insurance*

*Employer shall provide outpatient medical, major medical,
emergency medical evacuation, and dental insurance and professional care, through an internationally recognized company
or facility, acceptable to employee, for employee's and covered
dependents' medical and dental needs throughout the term of
the agreement, including all vacation and short leave periods,
on a twenty-four (24) hour per day basis. Such insurance and
medical or dental care shall be provided free of charge to the
employee and shall provide for coverage world wide. All medical treatment shall be by or under the direct supervision of an
expatriate doctor trained in the United States, Western Europe,
Australia, or country with equivalent standards of medicine.
Details of the coverage provided are contained in attachment I.*

Excellent medical care is often an employee's most important concern in developing countries. This is a serious matter and will require
professional advice, unless the employee happens to be a medical or
medical insurance professional. There will be more to say about medical care and insurance in the commentary to attachment I.

20. *Life Insurance*

*Employer shall provide, at no cost to the employee, term life
insurance covering employee and covered dependents during
the term of the agreement. Such insurance shall name the
employee and covered dependents as the insured (or those
insured) and shall further name the employee or employee's
next of kin as beneficiaries of the full amount of the coverage.
Details of this coverage are contained in attachment III. Proof
of coverage shall be handed over to the employee concurrent
with signing of the agreement.*

This is another subject that will require professional advice. In
some cases the employee may prefer to first agree on the types and

amounts of coverage with the employer, then obtain this through an agency in the employee's home country. The employee makes the payments directly and is compensated through expense reports. In this way the employee can be assured that the premium is paid on time and that the coverage doesn't lapse. There is more about this in the comments to attachment III.

21. Personal Accident Insurance

Employer shall provide, at no cost to employee, a personal accident insurance policy against any accident and/or injury and/or incapacity which employee may incur during the term of the agreement, whether job or non-job related, including coverage under the Workmen's Compensation Laws of (insert name of country here). Such coverage shall include a loss of income policy that provides for compensation to employee in an amount in U.S. dollars equal to two-thirds of employee's monthly base salary as shown in paragraph 3 of the employment agreement letter, per month of disability. The policy shall name the employee as the insured and shall further name the employee or employee's next of kin as beneficiaries of the full amount of the coverage. Refer to attachment III for further details of coverage. Proof of coverage has been handed over to the employee concurrent with signing of the agreement.

The comments following article 21 also apply to this article.

22. Death or Injury

In case of employee's death or injury, employer is to immediately notify employee's next of kin. In case of death of the employee and/or covered dependents, the body or bodies are to be embalmed and returned to employee's point of origin at employer's expense. In the event of employee's incapacitation or death, employer shall pay all outstanding amounts due, to the employee, covered dependents, or next of kin (as appropriate) and return the survivors and all personal effects to employee's point of origin as in articles 3, 7, 8, 13, and as otherwise provided for in the agreement.

This paragraph is self-explanatory. In case of death if some other disposition of the remains is preferred, such as cremation, then the wording will have to be changed.

Some preplanning and specific instructions to someone who could act on behalf of the employee and his or her dependents should be considered. This person should have the ability to think with a clear head under the pressure of the circumstances contemplated.

If the employee or a dependent has died it is understandable that the employer will want to finalize all matters as quickly as possible. Even if the employee has indicated a preference to be embalmed, the employer may suggest to the heirs that the remains be cremated instead of undergoing the expense of embalming and encapsulating in a sealed metal box as required by international health regulations. If cremation is the employee's preference anyway, then the only other factor to investigate is the facility available for this procedure.

Some developing countries have very modern crematories. These are usually available to the more well-to-do families. There will also be very simple facilities used by the poor that may be no more than a heavy steel plate resting on top of a brick fire pit, or similar facilities. Obviously there is a savings to be realized if the simple facilities are used. From the heirs' point of view, it is one experience to attend a modern facility and quite another where the remains are in full view throughout the procedure. Someone who is absolutely trusted should proceed to the crematorium with the remains ahead of the heirs and in sufficient time to insure that the preparations and method are as agreed to by the heirs.

23. Business Expenses

Only legitimate business expenses, including those for inoculations, annual or other employer authorized medical examinations, business travel and entertainment, laundry and subsistence while awaiting or seeking a permanent residence, taxis, auto rental, telephone, facsimile, telex, documented business entertainment at employee's residence, and similar costs incurred by employee will be paid for, or reimbursed, by the employer. In general, all air travel and temporary accommodations will be prepaid by the employer. All air travel for business purposes in the local operating area of the permanent residence place of less than two (2) hours scheduled duration will be tourist class. Employee shall be entitled to receive expense advances in amounts no less than the estimated cost of any business related entertainment, trip, or similar activity. Employee shall account for all business expenses in a form acceptable to employer no later than at the last working day of each calendar month. Employer shall reimburse employee for business expenses within seven (7) days of submission to employer.

Most employees, whether expatriate or native, understand that a business expense account is to be used solely for the benefit of their employer. Most employers accept the legitimate use of company funds by employees for business purposes, when these expenses are for activities within the guidelines established by the employer. On the basis of these two statements, the processing of expense accounts should be no more than a routine matter. However, to avoid misunderstandings, the employer's guidelines should be discussed in detail with the employee, prior to employment. The results of these discussions should be formulated into a memorandum of understanding, if the employer does not already have a written instruction. The employee should keep a copy, and a copy should be kept on file by the employer's chief financial officer. The contents should be reviewed and understood by all persons in accounting who may be involved in processing the employee's expense reports.

Discussions should include establishment of a budget for expenses, the amount of advance on expenses that the employee will normally be allowed to maintain outstanding, and how often expense accounts must be reconciled. In no case should it be necessary for the employee to use any significant amount of his or her own funds to finance legitimate business expenses except in unusual circumstances and then only for the few days needed for accounting to arrange reimbursement.

When first arriving, the employee may not have knowledge of local costs or the exact number and frequency of situations in which expenses will be incurred. Therefore, the budget should be reviewed frequently during the first six months of employment to determine adequacy and implement any modifications indicated.

The approval procedure for expense accounts should be clearly defined. In general, an employee incurs expenses as a result of carrying out assignments made or approved by his supervisor. The expenses may result from a specific instruction or a general requirement. A general requirement might be to entertain clients selectively but at the employee's discretion for the purpose of keeping them informed of the employer's products or services, or to obtain information useful to the employer.

The employee's immediate supervisor should be the one to judge whether or not the expenses incurred are reasonable and in the interest of the company. This judgment must be in line with the instructions the supervisor has given the employee *prior* to incurring expenses. If the *guidelines* for expense acceptability have to be modified, then changes should be made for *future* expenses, not after-the-fact for expenses already incurred and which are the result of previously agreed guidelines. Nor should judgment be left to a committee, a clerk in the accounting department, or anyone other than the employee's immediate supervisor.

Once the supervisor's approval is obtained, processing of the expense report and reimbursement should be routine and immediate. In general, there is no legitimate reason for reimbursement of expenses to be made later than one week after the expense report has been turned in by the employee. There is little that will do more to upset an employee (expatriate or native) who has sincerely tried to comply with the employer's guidelines and has submitted an expense report, than bureaucratic delays in receiving compensation.

If an employee has, for example, been on a business trip and in the course of that trip has cashed traveler's checks and has the receipts authenticating the transaction, then the exchange rate shown in that document should be the rate at which expenses in the currency in question are reimbursed. The argument that the exchange rate must be recalculated as of the day that the accounting clerk processes the expense report (because the rate is then in the company's favor and will thereby reduce the amount due the employee) is more destructive to the employee's motivation than the value to the employer of the few dollars saved.

Another expense topic that should be discussed is the purchase of alcoholic beverages for customers and business associates. Many employers in developing countries frown on or prohibit the use of alcohol because of their religious beliefs. If alcoholic beverages are allowed, it is still recommended that the employee be given a clear understanding of what type of support will be required in order to receive compensation. Especially to be avoided is the impression that the employee is simply buying drinks for himself or herself and using the business venue as a means of charging these to the employer. Such misunderstandings may result in the employee being asked to pay for all such entertainment out of his or her own pocket and being asked to justify the need with the accounting staff later on an item-by-item basis. The resulting discussions could be similar to an audit by the tax authorities with such questions as, why more than one drink? Why not cheaper drinks? Why not beer instead of mixed drinks? Why not locally blended scotch rather than imported? As often occurs in tax audits, the employee may finally agree to absorb some or all of the cost simply to get on with more important business.

To avoid such problems the employer and employee should discuss the employer's philosophy concerning the use of alcohol in detail beforehand. The employer should also explain to the employee if he or she has a direct reporting relationship to the accounting staff or if discussions concerning expenses should be through the employee's direct supervisor.

The employer should consider the *cost to benefit ratio* when establishing policies and procedures for incurring and reporting expenses. There is no question that such costs have to be controlled. However, the time spent by employees accounting and justifying expenses is also a cost to the employer that should be taken into account as well.

A project engineer, in charge of a multi-million dollar project, was summoned to the accounting department of his employer where he spent over an hour with an accounting clerk who insisted that the cost of a pack of cigarettes appearing on a lunch bill for customer entertainment be taken off the expense report because the employee couldn't prove that the cigarettes were actually for the customer, even though the employee didn't smoke. The engineer first tried to assure the clerk that the charge was legitimate. When this failed he tried unsuccessfully to show the clerk the ludicrous nature of the discussion since the cost per hour for the engineer's time while discussing the cigarettes far exceeded the cost of the cigarettes. The employee's supervisor finally intervened and the employee was reimbursed.

A native assistant-accounting manager made a $36.00 international telephone call to the finance manager who was on overseas business to get clarification on a $12.50 currency exchange item appearing on an employee's expense report.

In summary, the employer should explain the guidelines for business expenses and the relationship of the Finance and Accounting Department to the other functions in the company. Such guidance can help the employee avoid misunderstandings that might otherwise detract from the relationship.

24. Social and Business Clubs

Employer shall provide membership bonds (where applicable), monthly and/or annual fees for employee's and covered dependents' membership in no less than two (2) local organizations (to be selected by employee and approved by employer) such as a golf course, recreation, social or business club with facilities and programs for family as well as business entertainment. Employee shall pay all restaurant, bar, and other personal costs at these clubs that are not related to business entertainment.

This paragraph is self-explanatory. Obviously, the degree to which the employer should be willing to provide club membership will depend on the position that the employee is filling. If the employee is expected to entertain clients in executive positions, then membership in one or more clubs suitable for that purpose will be required. If, on the other hand, the employee is working as a technician within the employer's company and not expected to be in more than casual contact with clients, then membership would typically be provided in a club suitable for the employee's and dependents' personal use only. In such cases this would likely be the club catering to persons from the same country as the employee.

25. Use of Telephones

Personal long distance calls shall be borne by the employee except that employee may make a reasonable number of calls to the point of origin for purposes of maintaining contact with immediate family members during mobilization of employee's covered dependents and personal effects, and monthly after establishment of permanent residence at the location of the permanent residence place, for purposes of verifying the quality of care and maintenance of employee's residence at point of origin, the well-being of covered dependent children at boarding schools or universities, and other close relatives of employee and employee's spouse such as parents, brothers and sisters. Such telephone calls may be made by employee from any available telephone including but not limited to, employee's current residence (temporary or permanent), the employer's offices, a public telephone office, or other similar location.

In past years, telephones have been extraordinarily expensive to obtain and use in developing countries. Some progress has been made and the situation should continue to improve.

On one of my first permanent assignments overseas, in a developing country I had to arrange for five telephone lines. Each cost $1,000 in advance, and we had to wait two months before the first line was installed. It was another month before the remaining lines were in service.

A few weeks after the last was installed, the first line went dead. In the next two weeks, we lost two more lines and the next week the fourth. We were down to one line, which was totally inadequate for the type of work we were doing. Our local representative was at the phone company every day trying to get the lines fixed.

After much investigation we finally discovered the problem. It seems that the phone company had sold twice as many lines as they actually had available. They obviously made a lot of money this way at $1,000 per line (approximately 200,000 sold—100,000 available). New subscribers complained that they had paid a high price and did not have service after weeks of waiting. So, the phone company would disconnect a working line and reconnect it to the new subscriber who was then quite happy—until sometime later his line would be disconnected to appease another complaining customer.

After more investigation we found that the phone company technicians had only the bare essentials of hand tools with which to work. In our next shipment of supplies for the project, we imported 20 sets of telephone repairman's tools complete with belts and pouches. These were given to the phone company technicians. In addition, our purchasing agent would go each Friday to the phone company office with a large box of chocolates. These he passed out to each of the operators and their supervisors. Soon, all of our lines stayed connected and we had no problems with incoming or outgoing calls. In fact, the operators made it their duty to know where all of our key employees were, day and night, and never failed to track us down when an important call came in.

Years later, in another country, we had just moved our office from an old residence into a modern, new office building, complete with telephones that worked! Within one week all lines suddenly went dead. We found that the main underground trunk line serving our part of the city had been cut by an excavating machine. Hundreds of businesses had no telephone; several of the telephone company clients affected were embassies. In spite of the pressure put on the telephone company to speed up repairs, it was six months before we got our first line back. You can't always win.

In yet another situation, I had just arrived in the country and needed to meet with the employer's most important client. Fortunately, we had worked together many years previously. The city in this case was quite large with a population of over 7 million. The streets were filled to capacity from 6:30 A.M. to 7:00 P.M. I tried calling the client to make an appointment but had no luck the first two days. I decided to go early the next morning to his office without an appointment in hopes that he would have time to see me. After an hour in traffic, I arrived to discover that he was out of the city until the next day. I left a message and spent over an hour getting back to my office. The next day he tried to call me to no avail; I also tried to call him but still could not get through. In the end we finally met, one week after I started trying to make contact. This was at his club, and it was arranged entirely by handwritten messages carried by our respective drivers. We only made telephone contact weeks later.

The assignment of authority to use the telephone is a major difference found in developing countries. For example, it is common practice in some businesses that direct dial terminals are not allowed (even if they are available) because of possible misuse by staff. Typically, all calls must be placed through a company operator. In such companies there are seldom enough telephone lines or operators to handle the traffic efficiently. Connections that would take less than a minute to complete in a developed country may take hours, even a day or more, under such circumstances. It is also common that employees are not allowed to make any long-distance telephone calls without approval from higher authority.

The point is that in the process of "controlling" telephone expense, the operating efficiency of those employees who have an urgent and legitimate need is severely handicapped. It is also important that all calls, whether for business or personal need, be entered in a record book or by some similar method. This will help save time when reviewing charges received from accounting.

The home telephone can especially be a problem, since the invoice sent out by the telephone company very often makes little sense. Occasionally, the list of calls charged will not be correct. In some countries this creates a dilemma because if the invoice is not paid as received within a few days the service is disconnected. The procedure for correcting mistakes requires that the payment be made first and then a claim filed which will be investigated in due course. From a practical standpoint, one has little hope of recovering the funds. The extra cost can be substantial when the telephone company has incorrectly invoiced for a quantity of unaccountable overseas calls. The employer is in the best position to resolve such problems and should be responsible for the payment of all telephone services and any effort needed to rectify an incorrect invoice. The employee has little chance of obtaining a fair and rapid settlement of such matters. Of greater importance is the potential loss of time available for the employee to carry out the employer's assignments while negotiating with the telephone authorities. As previously recommended, the employee should keep a detailed log of all long distance calls made, whether for business or personal needs. If it is known that this is being done on a routine basis, there is less likelihood of charges being questioned.

26. Termination Due to Political or Civil Unrest

Should government rules or social conditions change, or should it become impractical or unsafe for the employee and/or covered dependents to remain in the country or geographic area of employment, in the opinion of the embassy or nearest consulate office of employee's country of origin, at any time, or in any other way whatsoever, then this agreement shall be terminated. The employee shall be entitled in such case to receive all benefits under the agreement including, but not limited to, all outstanding base pay, bonuses, vacation pay, short leave compensation, statement of taxes withheld, and other benefits that have accrued or will accrue up to the date employee can be expected to arrive at employee's point of origin (date to be agreed upon). Employee and covered dependents shall be returned, without prejudice, to employee's point of origin as in articles 3, 7, 8, 13, and 14, and as otherwise provided for in the agreement.

Most developing countries advertise their stability because this is a fundamental requirement for prospective foreign investors. However, this "apparent" stability may be the result of strong military or police organizations and may not represent the true feelings of the typical man on the street. The typical employee, on the other hand, will likely come from a country that has a relatively long history of political stability, or at least where civil discontent is resolved through political rather than military means. The employee has no way of controlling the political stability of the employer's country and should not be expected to endure any personal threat or assume any financial burden as a result of political or civil unrest that may develop.

This is a subject that should be examined thoroughly, especially by the employee. The possibility of suddenly having to leave the country should be planned in advance, especially with regard to the location and access to children's schools, the type and value of personal effects brought into the country, where bank accounts and important papers are kept, cash and credit cards available, maintenance of current exit visas, paid in advance airline tickets to country of origin, and so forth.

An employee manager working for a major multi-national company woke one day to find that a coup had occurred during the night and the entire country had been taken over by a new order. Although he had contacts in the new order and his wife spoke the local language fluently, the authorities refused to grant them permission to leave. After several days of house arrest and intense negotiating, word came that they could leave from the airport that afternoon but could only take one small suitcase for each family member and that could only contain personal clothing. In other words, all of their other personal effects were confiscated by the new authorities. Once the employee and family arrived in their country of origin, the employee submitted a claim to his employer's insurance department for the lost effects. To his surprise his claim was not only disallowed but he was informed that he no longer had a job since he could not return to his previous assignment and the employer had no other work available.

---

27. Termination by Employer

Employer may terminate the agreement only for cause which shall be defined as willful and deliberate conflicts of interest or willful neglect or refusal to perform legitimate duties for which employee is trained and experienced. Such termination shall be accomplished by giving sixty (60) days' written notice or two (2) months of the base pay amount as shown in paragraph 3 of the employment agreement letter in lieu of notice and returning employee and covered dependents to their point of origin as in articles 3, 7, 8, 13, and 14, and as otherwise provided for in the agreement. Employee shall not be entitled to receive any bonus amounts if terminated for cause.

The employee in most cases will be leaving an existing job in his or her country of origin for what is hoped will be a promising, if temporary, future in the developing country. The employee's decision to accept the position is of necessity based primarily on information from the employer.

The employer on his part will have to spend a considerable sum to find, interview, and transport the employee and dependents to the employer's country. At the same time, the employee's career as well as pocketbook will be substantially damaged if, after a few weeks or even months, the employer arbitrarily decides to terminate the agreement.

The term *arbitrarily* is used because if additional reasons for termination are included then it is not too difficult to identify some minor infraction that will fit such terminology. True, the employer will be out some cash if the employee doesn't work out but at least the employer's career has not likely been put in jeopardy. In so many words, the employee should not be hired on an off-the-cuff or arbitrary basis, nor should termination be an arbitrary decision. This is a serious matter for both parties and should be treated accordingly.

The employee is exposed and quite vulnerable under any other terms. The employer also benefits because his existing staff will be more keen to cooperate if they know the employee cannot be easily dismissed should he find a need to tread on sacred territory in order to accomplish an assignment made by the employer.

Often it is these islands of sacred territory that prompt the employer to seek outside help in the first place. The terms proposed in the agreement also make it important that the employer ensure the employee chosen has all of the capabilities needed for the position and that the support and resources the employee requires to carry out the job are available. What is intended is to achieve a "Win—Win" situation; the employee wants the job and the employer needs help. In such a situation, the language should be fair to both, not one-sided or onerous.

28. Termination by Employee

Employee may terminate this agreement by giving sixty (60) days written notice in which case employee may be required to work the remaining working days within that sixty (60) day period or, at employer's option, employer may pay the full sixty (60) days and terminate employee immediately. In either case employee shall receive all pay and benefits that have accrued under this agreement and employee and covered dependents shall be returned to their point of origin as in articles 3, 7, 8, 13, and 14, and as otherwise provided for in the agreement. Except in case of a material breach of the agreement on the part of the employer, employee shall not be entitled to receive any bonus amounts if the employee elects to terminate the agreement under this article 28. In case of a material breach on the part of employer, employee shall have the right to immediately terminate this agreement and claim full compensation, including bonuses and other benefits, as if the entire term of the agreement had been fulfilled.

The terms in this article are similar to the previous ones. The employee may truly believe, from what has been said and seen when visiting the proposed work location, that he or she will be able to perform the duties contemplated and achieve satisfaction in the new job. However, it is impossible for the employer and employee to discuss all facets of the employer's business, especially personalities that the employee will eventually work with daily. If, after a few months experience in the employer's organization the employee realizes that it is unlikely that he or she will be able to achieve the goals discussed in pre-job interviews, then it is likely that neither the employee or employer will want to continue the relationship. This is not likely to be a snap decision on the employee's part but one that may have to made.

The wording of this paragraph provides a fair and equitable means of ending the arrangement in such circumstances. If the terms were more onerous, and the employee stayed on simply to complete the term of the agreement, neither the employee nor employer would likely receive the benefit for which either bargained.

29. Statements to the Media

Employee agrees, except with prior written consent of employer, not to make directly or indirectly any statement publicly whether to the press or in books, magazines, periodicals, by advertisement, radio, television, film or any other means, concerning matters relative to the operations or financial aspects of employer, any company or organization with whom employer is working, or concerning matters of a political nature which might impair the relations of the employer with employer's customers, subcontractors or any other companies, affiliations, national entities or other organizations with whom employer relies upon or does business. This paragraph shall not apply to information that is generally considered to be in the public domain.

The employee simply cannot make statements to the press or others outside of the employer's organization, about the employer's confidential business affairs, without the employer's express (written) permission.

30. Extension of the Agreement

In case it is mutually agreed to extend the agreement, for any period of time, or for any reason what-so-ever, all terms and benefits of the agreement shall continue throughout the extension period as if no break in the agreement had occurred except that any bonuses due employee at the end of the primary agreement period will be paid as scheduled. Any time spent by employee waiting to receive final payment shall be considered an extension of the agreement.

It is unlikely that the employer will be able to plan his work so precisely that the employee will be able to depart exactly on the date shown in the employment agreement. Therefore, there needs to be language in the agreement that covers the eventuality of an extension.

31. Entire Agreement

The agreement, which is defined as those documents entitled "employment agreement letter", the "conditions of employment" and "attachments" I, II, III, IV, V, and VI thereto, embodies the entire agreement between employer and employee and, except as noted below, supersedes all previous verbal and written communications between the parties. Headings, titles and punctuation used in the agreement are for convenience only. Each article of the agreement shall be read and interpreted in conjunction with each and all other articles of the agreement. Neither employer or employee makes any representations, warranties or guaranties, expressed or implied, other than those expressly set forth in the agreement. The agreement shall not be amended except in writing and signed by the waiving party.

Any work undertaken by employee on behalf of employer prior to the execution of the agreement shall be deemed to have been carried out under and pursuant to the agreement which shall form the basis of all compensation and benefits due employee for such work done. Such work shall include, but is not limited to, employee's time following resignation from an existing job for the express purpose of entering the employment of employer, packing of employee's personal effects in preparation to relocate to the permanent residence place as shown in paragraph 9 of the employment agreement letter, acting for or on behalf of employer in any business or social function and/or any other similar activity that employee undertakes based on a letter of understanding or similar device prepared on the employer's letterhead stationary that would indicate the intention of employer to employ employee.

The two paragraphs above should be easily understood. The situation described in the second paragraph is often overlooked.

32. Interpretation

The agreement is to be interpreted in the English language and under the laws of the country of (name of the country and state agreed to). Any disputes which may arise during the term of the agreement between the parties that cannot be resolved amicably, shall be arbitrated under the rules of the (U.S. Chamber of Commerce, or other organization as agreed to). The employee shall at all times have the right to seek professional, legal, and financial council in resolving matters of disagreement concerning the terms of the agreement and such aid or advice shall not serve to prejudice employee's continued employment under the agreement or be deemed a conflict of interest.

The language and concept described above should be easily understood and need no further explanation.

33. Compliance with Law

Both employer and employee shall comply with all applicable laws of the countries in which the employee is required to work under the agreement.

Again, the language and concept described above should be easily understood and need no further explanation.

35. Clarifications

Should any provision(s) of the agreement be judged unlawful, in any country where the employer may require the employee to work, then the parties shall meet and, in good faith, resolve and agree on alternate language which shall have the same or equivalent meaning as the original, and which complies with the laws of the country in question. In no case shall the net amounts due employee ever be less than the amounts shown in the employment agreement letter as a result of such clarifications.

3

Attachment I: Medical Examinations, Insurance, and Medical Records

1. Initial and Annual Medical Examinations

As a condition of employment employee agrees to undergo a comprehensive physical examination at a medical clinic and by a physician approved by the employer. Employee further agrees to undergo a medical examination once each year and at the end of or termination of the agreement. Each covered dependent shall also comply with this requirement. Employer will provide the forms required for all examinations either directly or through the examining physician. Employer will pay all costs of examinations, lab and special tests, and other charges associated with or relating to these examinations. The original copy of medical examination reports shall be transmitted by the examining physician directly to the employer and a copy to the employee. All original medical records shall be the property of employer.

Anyone with a medical condition should not consider moving to a developing country without the approval of a physician who is knowledgeable about the health conditions and availability of any special medical care the employee may need in that country. No employer wants to hire an employee who has a condition that does or may detract from the employee's performance. This also applies to the employee's dependents, since time may be required away from the job to tend to a dependent who is chronically ill.

Both the employee and employer will want to ensure that the employee and dependents remain in good health. Therefore, the initial and all following physical examinations need to be comprehensive. "Comprehensive" means a *complete* analysis of the employee's and dependents' health profiles. In addition to looking into eyes, ears, nose, and throat, coughing left and right, listening to and thumping the chest, feeling the abdomen, checking reflexes and the full use of limbs and joints, the examination should also include no less than:

- Complete blood analysis.
- Stool analysis.
- Chest x-rays.
- Urinalysis.
- Electrocardiogram (usually for adults only).
- Perhaps a stress test for specific individuals.
- Obviously, any additional test(s) the examining physician believes appropriate for a particular individual (e.g., verification that an individual who has a history of kidney stones does not currently have any).

The employee should ask the physician about any special care needed to avoid parasites. Each year all family members should be examined for parasites, especially in the tropics.

The employee and dependents will want a thorough dental checkup, teeth cleaned, and all corrective work completed before leaving their country of origin. This work will (probably) not be paid for by the prospective employer while he should pay for the cost of physical examinations.

The employee should consider buying several good medical reference books to take with him to his new assignment. A list of these will be found in sources of information for employees at the end of the book.

2. Immunization

Employee and covered dependents agree to be immunized as recommended by the attending physician.

I am not a physician, so I can only comment from my own experience. There seems to be wide medical opinion concerning the necessity to be immunized for all of the possible diseases the employee and dependents might be exposed to in overseas travels. Diseases still common in some developing countries include typhus, tetanus, diphtheria, hepatitis 'A' and 'B' and others. In at least one Southeast Asia country it has been reported that approximately 25%

of the population are carriers of hepatitis 'B.' Ultimately, what immunizations are administered is a decision between the individual and the attending physician.

3. Medical Examinations and the Employer's Rights

The employer shall have the right to act on the recommendations of the attending physician with regard to employee's initial or continued employment, as appropriate.

Should a prospective employee fail the pre-employment examination due to a condition that can be corrected, the prospective employee may undergo corrective treatment and submit to re-examination by an employer approved physician. Both the corrective treatment and re-examination costs shall be borne by the prospective employee. Employer shall notify the prospective employee in writing of the date by which such corrective treatment and re-examination by employer's physician must be completed in order for the prospective employee to remain eligible for employment.

I don't believe this needs explanation. The employer must be able to make the final decision concerning the fitness of anyone he intends to employ or the continuation of their employment, should they become unfit due to a medical condition. If the insurance policies mentioned in the agreement are planned carefully, in place, and the premium payments up to date, then the employee will be protected, to the limit spelled out in the applicable policy, should he or she become unable to work due to a medical condition that develops after employment.

4. Covered Dependent Failure of Medical Examination

Should the attending physician recommend against one or more covered dependents being domiciled in the permanent residence place, then the employee may choose a nonfamily status or make arrangements for care of the dependent (or dependents) in employee's country of origin, or elsewhere, at employee's sole discretion and expense. In this event, any or all such dependents shall be removed from the list of covered dependents and shall not be eligible for any dependent benefits under the agreement.

This is similar to paragraph 3 above. The employee will not likely want to take a dependent to or keep the dependent in a location where there is risk due to a medical condition.

I know of one family that was examined in their country of origin and considered to be in excellent health. Within days of arrival at their new assignment, they discovered that one of their children was allergic to a local plant. This was a surprise because the child had never experienced an allergic reaction before. By the third week the child had to be emergency evacuated out of the country because breathing became almost impossible due to swelling in her throat.

5. Location of Examining Clinic

It is intended that all medical examinations will be carried out in the employee's country and city of origin. Annual examinations should be conducted during annual vacation, at the same facility, and by the same physician as the initial examinations, wherever possible. Where this is not feasible, employer shall designate the city and clinic where examinations are to be taken. Should this city be located more than three (3) hours distance by automobile from employee's residence in country of origin, employer will arrange and pay for round trip transportation to and from the designated city, accommodations, food, and rental auto (or taxi, as applicable). All such costs will be arranged on the basis of direct billing to employer.

The wording used here will probably be applicable to most employee employment situations. A benefit to the employer of having the employee examined, at least initially, in his or her country of origin is that the employer will save the cost of transporting the prospective employee (and dependents) to the permanent residence place, should the employee or a dependent fail the examination. On the other hand, the employer may prefer the examinations conducted at a clinic he normally uses in his own country. There are excellent clinics in some developing countries (or a neighboring country) that are as well staffed, equipped, and capable as their counterparts in developed countries. The cost of equivalent examinations in these clinics is generally less than in a developed country (except where it is free). I have experience over a number of years in using clinics in such countries and, in my opinion, these particular clinics were professional in all respects.

If the employer does want the prospective employee to be examined in his country of origin, and neither has a preferred physician, the employee (or the employer) should locate a physician that has knowledge of medical facilities and health conditions in the employer's country. I mention this because it is my experience that physicians, in my home country at least, do not all have sufficient knowledge of conditions in developing countries to know what to look for or how to advise the employee. Knowledge appears to be especially lacking with respect to tropical diseases and the many parasites and viruses that can be encountered.

One way to locate a physician with the needed qualifications might be through the local medical referral agency found in most large cities. Employees living in the intended country would obviously be a good source of advice; multinational companies with operations in the country could be asked the name of the physicians they use.

6. Time and Compensation during Medical Examinations

After employment, employee will be allowed up to three (3) days in which to complete each annual medical examination. Employee will be compensated for the actual days utilized in taking these examinations on the same basis as paid annual vacation as described in paragraph 16 of the conditions of employment. Prior approval from the employer shall be required for any extension beyond the three (3) day limit. Any extension shall be based on the written recommendation of the attending physician.

This is self-explanatory .

7. Medical Insurance

There must be a paragraph here concerning medical insurance coverage. This should include at least the:

- *Name, address, telephone, and facsimile number of each company providing coverage.*
- *Policy number(s) and date(s) of document(s).*
- *Name of the document(s) that lists the benefits provided by the policy including what is paid by the employer and what costs (or proportions thereof), if any, the employee is expected to pay.*
- *Date that coverage(s) becomes effective.*
- *Date by which the policy(s) must be renewed.*

- *Name of the insurance company('s) representative(s) to contact for clarifications, if required.*

The employee should receive a copy of each policy, usually in the form of a booklet, which describes the coverage in detail, including but not limited to, a list of medical procedures and illnesses and the amount that the insurance company will pay for each, the procedures to follow in reporting an injury or illness, the method by which claims will be processed at the permanent residence place and when the employee and covered dependents are traveling or otherwise remote from the permanent residence place. One method of establishing the benefits that should be contained in the medical insurance package is to contact multi-national companies with offices in the country of interest and obtain a copy of the package provided for their expatriate employees.

The employee should receive identification cards from the employer or insurance companies for employee and each person named as a covered dependent. In addition to the name of the person to whom the card is issued, this card should list the name of the insurance company, the policy number, the insurance company's address, and telephone number to call on a 24-hour basis for verification of coverage, and facsimile number. In addition, the insurance company may require treatment while employee or covered dependents are physically in the permanent residence place be obtained through a specific clinic. If this is the case then the telephone numbers for both normal work day and after hours calls and the clinic address should be shown on the card.

The employee must analyze the policy to ensure that sufficient coverage has been provided, that the coverage is applicable worldwide, and does not exclude employee's country of origin or the United States. The usual medical insurance may or may not include coverage for emergency medical evacuation. Such coverage may have to be provided as a separate policy.

The first part of this is self-explanatory. Most employees will already have experience with medical insurance whether provided by their home country employer or as part of a national health plan. The essentials will be similar. An area that will probably not be the same is emergency medical evacuation insurance. By emergency medical evacuation is meant transportation of the patient to the nearest facility that can provide the type of care required, either in-country or in another country.

At the time of this writing, medical insurance policies that include coverage for emergency medical evacuation were available to persons living in most developing countries. However, even with such insurance the employee may not have a say in selecting an *appropriate* facility for treatment. In some countries it is only the attending physician who can make this decision, regardless of the terms of the policy.

There is also the possibility that this decision may be made more on the basis of nationalistic pride than considerations of the patient's welfare. By sending the patient to another country, the physician will be admitting that his country does not yet meet the standards required. Also, his country cannot obtain "experience" if patients are allowed to choose facilities in another country. More about this later.

There is another type of emergency medical evacuation service available. These are companies that provide emergency medical aid as well as land and air evacuation.

The difference between the two plans may need clarification because at first glance they appear to provide similar coverage. The first is primarily an *insurance* company that provides reimbursement for all or a portion of medical costs. These companies do not provide medical treatment. The policy holder has to find his own doctor, arrange for payments and refunds, and so forth, as one would expect with any private medical insurance plan.

The second type of company is primarily a *medical organization* that has clinics in many developing nations. Medical care is available on a membership basis only. Membership fees cover the cost of emergency medical evacuation up to the dollar limit chosen by the member when purchasing the policy. The cost of outpatient care at the clinics is charged separately and is in addition to membership fees. These outpatient costs may or may not be covered by the first type of insurance.

There are usually several levels of coverage available under the emergency evacuation plan provided by the second type of company. This allows the member to choose coverage that closely approximates his or her particular circumstances. For example, if the member is living in a large city with international flights leaving daily to countries where more advanced medical facilities are available, then the cost of evacuation would likely be minimal. On the other hand, the member may live in some remote camp, two hours by helicopter to the nearest dirt airstrip from which a charter aircraft would be required to reach the nearest international airport, perhaps several hours distance. With the cost of such services being hundreds of dollars per hour, it is easy to see that the charges could soon become substantial. Hence, the amount of coverage needed for the second example would be greater. Companies (or clinics) providing this service have staff familiar with conditions in their area who can provide guidelines to aid the new member in choosing the optimum coverage for his or her particular circumstances.

The clinics are usually part of a chain or larger group of such facilities. Each clinic is established by expatriate doctors who carefully research the needs and existing capabilities of the specific location. The doctors and nurses staffing these facilities are normally native personnel who have been carefully screened by the expatriate doctors who established the clinic.

All insurance companies should provide members with identification cards which give emergency instructions in the local language. One improvement that has been suggested (but to my knowledge not yet adapted) is to offer the member the option of having his or her identification card in a form suitable for suspending around the neck on a chain so that it is less likely to be left at home, lost, or stolen. This would be especially applicable to younger children, since it is not practical for them to carry wallets or purses.

8. Medical Records to Be Kept Confidential

Employer agrees to keep all employee and covered dependents medical records confidential and in locked files available only to the chief executive of employer or his designated representative.

This paragraph is also self-explanatory. For example, no one cares to walk into the employer's personnel office (unexpectedly) and find their personal medical records being reviewed and discussed by an assortment of clerks, not all of whom are from the personnel department.

Locally Available Medical Care

Even outside of the special clinics mentioned previously, there are many native doctors who are every bit as competent as their counterparts in the developed world. This is a layman's opinion based on my own personal experience as well as that of friends. Most people want a physician who can communicate, who displays genuine concern for the patient, sincerely cares for his or her welfare, and who has the professional ability to get results. These qualities are not limited to medical practitioners in developed countries.

Perhaps the major difference in a developing country is that the theoretical and practical requirements needed to practice medicine are not always as strictly controlled as in developed nations. At the same time, this can only be a relative statement because there are sufficient cases to indicate that some improvement in the medical profession in developed nations is still needed, even in countries with the most advanced medical technology. As in the developed nations, the best doctors achieve that distinction through years of study and experience and are generally found through referrals rather than out of a telephone book.

Getting Involved Ensures Good Health

The employee just arriving in an unfamiliar environment has to be more alert, perhaps get more directly involved in health concerns than he or she would at home.

The employee has recently arrived and is still living in the hotel. This is a four-star hotel, part of an international chain, managed at the top by expatriate staff, and (apparently) reliable in all respects. It's the kind of hotel where you would feel quite safe and well cared for the minute you walked in the door.

Within a month of arrival a young family member suddenly comes down with diarrhea and nausea; the usual flu remedies have no effect. That evening the hotel is asked to send for a doctor. The doctor arrives shortly. Medicine is prescribed and administered. By the next morning there is no improvement; in fact, the patient is getting worse. The employee talks directly with the hotel general manager, who is also an expatriate, who promises that the best doctor in the area will be summoned. The new doctor arrives and prescribes yet a different treatment. Throughout the day no improvement is seen. Another doctor comes in the evening and prescribes new medication.

By the third morning the child is very sick. No one needs medical training to know this. The employee is now extremely concerned about the survival of the child. He has a more aggressive discussion with the hotel management (an understatement).

Another doctor arrives. He very quickly diagnoses that the patient has a classic case of dysentery and that the prior treatment prescribed had no hope of curing it. He explains that the medicines already prescribed were no more than over-the-counter cold remedies in developed countries. He administers treatment, and the next day the patient is feeling and looking better. In another two days, he returns to school. (I can verify this story. The patient was my son.)

Several years later, while recuperating from an operation in a very good hospital in Southeast Asia, I met a middle-aged woman in the ward waiting room. She had just flown in from overseas to look after a niece who had been in an accident. When I asked about the accident, she pulled out a photo of two smiling men in white medical jackets in front of what appeared to be an aid station and related the following:

The niece arrived at the entrance to the same hospital I was in late at night several days previously. The taxi driver set her back pack next to her. A staff orderly stepped outside to see what was going on. The young woman was almost incoherent but managed to explain that she had just arrived after an eight-hour flight from a well-known vacation island. She was obviously in pain and very sick. She said her right arm was broken. It was bandaged and in a makeshift sling. The color of her hand was dark red. She was rushed to emergency. After several hours, she was out of emergency and in her room. The next afternoon she told the following story:

She had flown over 10,000 miles during her school's spring break to a certain tropic isle noted for its surf. She came alone. On the third day and while surfing, she was slammed to the bottom when a wave broke over her. Her right hand hit the bottom and the shock caused the break between the wrist and elbow.

Luckily, she had met other young people during her first day on the island. They saw the accident and got her out of the water. After the initial shock, she was able to stand and walk. A taxi was located, and she was taken to a first-aid station several miles away. There wasn't a hospital on the island, although thousands of visitors come each year from all over the world.

The aid station was manned by two persons. Neither spoke the young woman's native language (English). One of her newly made friends went out on the street and found a person who could interpret. After a few exchanges, the aid people understood the problem. The pain was becoming more intense. There was more discussion.

The interpreter explained that the two aid workers noticed the camera the young woman had around her neck. They insisted they all go outside and that she take their picture in front of the aid station. She wanted them to look at her arm. They continued to insist until the whole party finally went out on the street and the picture was taken.

Back inside they began to work on her arm. After initial examination they explained that she should simply not use the arm until it had healed; there was no attempt to provide a splint or even offer a sling. They had no suggestion where she should go for further care. By now she was in considerable pain.

Her recently made friends insisted that the aid workers do more. Finally, they produced a makeshift sling (still no splint). While they put her arm in the sling, she fainted from pain as the arm was moved from its suspended position. After a few moments of heated exchanges between the young woman's friends and the aid workers, one of the aid workers produced a syringe and injected a pain killer. In a few minutes the woman woke and was still in great pain, but she was able to get up off the cot where she had been placed. A friend paid the aid workers and the party left.

The young woman was taken back to her hotel. The pain killer was starting to take effect, and she had to be helped into bed. She fainted again from the pain as her arm came to its new position. During the night one of her friends watched over her. Early in the evening, they became concerned because of her deep sleep. At times she seemed to stop breathing. One of her friends went back to the aid station to find out what she had been injected with. However, the aid station was closed. Throughout the first night, they constantly talked to her, concerned that she might stop breathing.

The next morning a friend went back to the aid station. There were two new people there. One spoke some English. The woman's condition was explained. One of the aid workers agreed to come to the hotel to see if there was anything that could be done.

Back at the hotel the young woman was still in a deep sleep. The aid worker examined her arm. It was terribly swollen and discolored. The aid worker had brought some bandages, wrapped the arm, and eased it back into the sling. One of the woman's friends suggested that the bandage was too tight. The aid worker insisted the arm would now get better and left.

In the early evening the woman began to wake. The arm hurt and her hand was quite swollen, puffy, and the color deepening. She was finally awake enough to ask that one of her friends make arrangements for her to fly out to the nearest hospital. The earliest flight was mid-morning the next day. Later that evening her hand was in so much pain that she asked her friends to loosen the bandage. Again, she fainted in the process. That night she did seem to sleep more comfortably. The next morning she was escorted to the plane, and after eight hours and two stops she arrived at the hospital.

The bottom line is that one's health and access to *professional* medical care (as that term is defined in developed countries) should be a serious concern to the employee, the employee's dependents, and the employer. As can be seen from the previous examples, the employee and dependents are the most vulnerable to medical emergencies in the early days and weeks of their arrival, before having had a chance to locate sources of professional medical care.

The employee is sometimes surprised at the (apparent) laid-back attitude of people in developing countries about injury, sickness, poor medical care, life, and death. It isn't that these people care less about their families (or the employee), but simply that they have made the mental adjustment needed to keep one's wits to survive in an environment over which they have very little control or expertise. Typical characteristics of this environment are:

- Crowded living conditions
- General lack of public knowledge about bacteria, viruses, and hygiene
- Poor or nonexistent potable water and sanitary gathering and disposal systems
- Use of night soil for fertilizing food crops
- Inappropriate use of chemicals for crop protection
- Contaminated streams, rivers, and bays
- Geographic and climatic conditions that promote the breeding of pests and the diseases they carry

These conditions result in higher infant mortality rates and shorter life spans as compared to developed nations. The native population knows that there will frequently be a family member or close friend who is sick or who dies. It's a situation that is not any more acceptable in these countries than it would be in developed nations, but it's one that the local population has to live with on a day-to-day basis. The employee has to live and survive in this same environment.

Local authorities are trying to improve these conditions. However, it will take time to accomplish, especially where the population is expanding more rapidly than public utilities and the health care system. In metropolitan areas where the number of expatriates has been substantial over an extended period, the health care available will generally be better. If the household staff have worked previously for employees their knowledge of hygiene will probably, but not always, be better.

Hygiene and the Household Staff

In some locations, the community has set up organizations that teach household staff the fundamentals of hygiene. Typically, they also provide cooking lessons and explain recipes from many developed countries. Finding a cook that has worked for expatriates from a variety of countries can be a real bonanza both to one's health and gastronomic interests.

If the location isn't well developed then the employee must be prepared to teach even the most fundamental principals of hygiene. However, one can never relax about hygienic matters, although the household staff has been trained and appears to understand what is expected.

An employee, with wife and two small children, was working for a multinational company in a relatively sophisticated village built by their employer. They had a household staff that had been with them more than three years. The staff had been trained in hygiene in a special school by the employer.

One weekend the employee and wife decided to stay overnight at the company cottage at a nearby beach. They had done this before and felt quite comfortable leaving the children in the care of the household staff.

While they were away, the house boy, thinking he would please by doing some of the tasks that the employee normally called the maintenance people to do, took the water filter apart to see if it needed replacement. To him it looked muddy and rusty. But when he went to the cupboard to find a new one there was none in the usual place. Since the filter only *appeared* to be coated with mud and rust he reasoned that if he simply cleaned it off he could then put it back in the system and all would be well.

There wasn't a brush normally used for this purpose, so he chose the best he could find for the job. It was the one used to clean off the employee's field boots. Soon after the children drank some of the water passing through the filter, they became ill. A neighbor drove to the beach to fetch the employee and his wife. Ultimately, one of the children died and one recovered. The household staff became only slightly ill since their systems were better programmed to the environment.

Hygiene is a subject that people in (most) developed nations have learned over many years of practical experience supported by disciplined research. In the developed world, hygiene is expected to be a part of daily life both at home and at work. On the other hand, the individual in a developing nation who is likely to seek a job as household staff may not practice the same level of hygiene at home as he or she is taught and required to follow at work. For instance, washing hands and the care in the handling of food are practices that the employee thinks are important, but a staff member may not fully comprehend, even after receiving formal training. Therefore, when a new application for a previously learned hygienic principle is encountered, the staff member may not immediately see the connection.

People in developing nations are certainly as capable mentally as their developed world brethren. It is a mistake to think otherwise. The difference with subjects such as hygiene is that the principles are still being assimilated into their daily lives. With education and time this will change. In the meantime, the expatriate's family must be explicit with instructions concerning hygiene and be constantly alert for errors.

Getting Approvals for Emergency Medical Evacuation

Another aspect of health care that the employer and employee should discuss is the policy or attitude of the local government and medical authorities about evacuation for medical treatment outside the country. There seems to be a great variation in what to expect, depending on the particular nation.

Some countries are quite lenient and readily allow emergency medical evacuations, while others will not want to provide the necessary exit permit since, in their opinion, local facilities and medical care are adequate. What we are talking about here is pride and nationalism overcoming concern for the welfare of the patient. There may also be the desire to keep patients in the country in order to give local medical staff additional experience.

In some countries it may even be a crucial decision to take a patient to a local hospital, since once checked in it may become difficult to impossible to move the patient for the same reasons previously mentioned. Where the patient has membership in the local medical clinic supervised by expatriate doctors (as described earlier), he or she is usually advised not to even call for local ambulance service, since they may refuse to take the patient to any medical facility other than a specific hospital with which they have a contract.

Many years ago one of our employees developed stomach pains and was taken to the one and only local hospital. The construction of this facility had been started many years before but had never been completed due to lack of funds. In fact, only the concrete structure was in place; there were no doors, windows, screens, electricity, plumbing, or similar items. Oil lamps were used for lighting.

Our man was placed in a third-story room and under substantial sedation, since he was in rather great pain. Another employee stayed with him all night but early in the morning had gone to the ground floor to find some coffee. He got his coffee and was walking back up the stairs when he suddenly heard his friend screaming.

Racing up the stairs and fearing that his friend was in even more desperate pain, he ran into the room to find in the first glow of daylight two large vultures perched in the window and one on the foot of his friend's steel framed bed; they were critically studying the patient! The sick employee had been wakened by the rustling sounds of the vultures' feathers. Still being quite groggy from the sedation, he half-dreamed he had been assumed dead and his body put out for the scavengers to feed on, a practice not uncommon in the particular country.

Health Care for the Household Staff

Another health care problem of the employee concerns the native household staff. In many locations it is possible to obtain a workmen's compensation-type insurance for such staff. This may even be required by local law. Therefore, if an individual is injured, he or she may be eligible for treatment at an indigenous hospital and collect limited income benefits, if the injury or sickness is serious and long lasting.

However, many expatriates prefer more personal care for staff, since they often become almost like part of the family. For this reason, it is usually not difficult to find a well-qualified native doctor who is willing to accept household staff outpatients.

On the other hand, some staff may have a real fear of modern medical practice and prefer to go to a healer in their home village. The point is that the expatriate should investigate local possibilities and solutions for such situations before they occur, should determine what is technically best for the staff, and at the same time keep within each individual's wishes. In any case, it is wise to have any sickness diagnosed first by a contemporary medical practitioner because of the possibility of a serious communicable disease.

Being Cautious about Lab Work and Reports

Having made the above statement, it is necessary to caution that laboratory work is not always carried out under the best of conditions or with the expertise that is necessary for sound professional interpretation. Such work should be confirmed through repeated tests, preferably at different labs (in the rare circumstance where there is more than one) before any serious steps such as surgery are approved. This is not to say that hospitals do not have the most modern equipment and facilities; it says only that the level of expertise with which it is used may not be up to the level of the equipment in all cases. Although hopefully rare, the reports of lab tests could be influenced by the personal beliefs of the lab technician conducting the tests.

An indigenous family had adopted a two-month-old baby. The child seemed sickly and was taken to the family's pediatrician who practiced in one of the best local clinics. Several tests were run but nothing was reported that would account for the condition of the child. The doctor tried various prescriptions but the child remained ill.

After several months the husband had to travel to a nearby country where, coincidentally, medical facilities were more sophisticated. It was decided that his wife and the adopted infant would accompany him and the child taken to a doctor for additional diagnosis. To their surprise the foreign clinic immediately determined that the child had syphilis! Several more tests were run to be sure of the results. All proved the same.

On return to their home country the situation was reported to the family doctor. He was very upset and personally went to the lab to examine the records. The original lab tests did indicate syphilis, but it was not shown on the report received by the doctor. The technician who had run the tests was confronted with the evidence. The technician acknowledged the original results but said that the syphilis was not reported because people of the child's religion simply did not engage in the type of immoral activity that might lead to contracting such a disease. Therefore, there had to be an error in the tests, so the results weren't reported.

Nursing Care for the Patient

If one does end up in a local hospital, perhaps the most critical need besides a good doctor and reliable lab work will often be professional nursing care.

Let's say that an excellent local doctor has been found and the patient has survived the necessary procedure. The doctor prescribes certain medicines at specific times. Unless there is a family member in the room at all times to verify that the right medicines are being administered at the right times, there is the chance that they won't.

There will probably be one or two professionally trained nurses available who are excellent but who obviously can't be everywhere at once or even closely supervise the junior staff. Therefore, the patient's family are expected to carry out many of the routine duties performed by nurses in hospitals in developed countries such as changing linen, cleaning the patient, and fetching water. It's because of the uncertainties of post-operative care and the possibility of non-sterile conditions outside of the operating room that make surgery in many developing countries hazardous in spite of the availability of excellent doctors and operating facilities.

4

Attachment II: Employee's Instruction to Payroll

The following are the employee's instructions for the distribution of employee's monthly base salary and bonus amounts:

1. The portion of monthly base salary paid each month to employee at the permanent residence place is to be: US $_____.

    This amount is to be in the form of: (Employee to choose/initial one)

    Traveler's checks _____   Cash _____

2. The remainder of monthly base salary in the amount of US $_____ is to be sent by wire transfer to:

    Account name: _____

    Account number: _____

    Name of bank: _____

    Branch: _____

    City: _____

    State: _____

    Country: _____

    Telex no.: _____

3. Employee's bonus is to be paid as in paragraph (1 or 2) _____ above when due.

Monthly base salary payments (in travelers' checks or cash) will be made on the last day of each calendar month or nearest working day, should the last day fall on a weekend.

Funds being wire transferred will be processed by employer so that they arrive in employee's account before the end of the calendar month due. Employer will furnish employee a copy of the bank's confirmation of the date and the amount of the funds transferred. The employer will pay all cost of wire transfers.

Approved by employee: **Received on behalf of employer by:**

Signature: _____   Signature: _____

Name typed: _____   Name Typed: _____

Date: _____   Date: _____

This attachment provides specific instructions for disposition of the employee's monthly pay and bonus amounts. The intent is to eliminate misunderstandings and mistakes.

The first paragraph concerns the funds that the employee will need each month for local living and miscellaneous expenses. If the employee is new to the area, then it is likely that the initial amount selected will have to be adjusted up or down after a few months to fit *actual* needs. In this case, a new form should be filled out and signed by both parties.

Whether to receive funds for local use in the form of traveler's checks or cash is a personal decision. Traveler's checks are recommended because they are safer to carry. If traveler's checks are chosen, they should be issued by a bank from which traveler's checks are well known and generally accepted worldwide, not just in the country in which they are issued.

In the second paragraph, the employee must be sure that the information asked for is entered correctly the first time—then check it again to be sure. Before leaving his or her country of origin, the employee should obtain a complete understanding of the telegraphic-transfer process from his bank. To achieve this he should make an appointment with the officer at the bank responsible for handling these transactions. A list of questions should be prepared before the appointment. Listed below are typical questions that should be asked:

- What route will the wire transfer take between the employer's bank and this bank? To respond to this, the employee's banker will need at least the name and address of the employer's bank and the name of their corresponding bank in the employee's home country. The employer should be able to provide this information.

- Does the employee's bank charge for handling funds that are received through telegraphic transfer? There should not be a charge, but some banks will charge for it. If the bank does, it can add up to a substantial amount over a period of years. The employer should give instructions to his bank that the employee's funds are to arrive in his account free of all transfer charges.

- Will there be any delay in depositing the funds in the employee's account? Will there be a delay in his or her ability to write checks on the funds deposited once they reach the bank? If so, why and for how long?

- If the employee has set up automatic payments from his checking account, will the bank allow an overdraft if a delay occurs in receipt of funds? If so, how much? Will there be a charge for it?

- Who should be contacted at the bank if it becomes necessary for the employee to do so while overseas?

- Does the bank have a special facsimile or telex number that should be used if communications become necessary?

The employee should leave his or her overseas telephone, facsimile, and telex numbers with the bank officer, in case the bank finds an urgent need to communicate. The employee may want the bank to confirm each receipt of funds by facsimile or telex.

Moving Funds as Quickly and Safely as Possible

At the time of this writing, the fastest method of moving funds from one bank to another was by "telegraphic transfer." This is sometimes also referred to as "wire transfer." If the employee has not had previous experience with "telegraphic transfers," it is important to know that although this is currently the fastest method of transferring funds, it is not advisable to "assume" that each transaction will take place as planned. For example, banks will sometimes hold funds being transferred in their own account while at the same time telling the person who is waiting on the money that "It hasn't arrived yet." Telegraphic transfers are not always directly between the two principal banks. More often the funds will pass through several banks before reaching the final destination. Therefore, it's also possible that the funds may be delayed by one or more of the banks in the communications link between the employer's and employee's banks.

When a transfer is delayed or can't be accounted for, it is likely that a bank in the chain has put the funds in the short-term money market for the purpose of garnering interest for their own account. A sizable amount of income can be derived if enough transfers are delayed this way.

This is nothing less than a "legal" form of embezzlement, since the banks are using the property (money) of others that has been entrusted to their care for their own gain without the knowledge of the rightful owners. Banks that charge the depositor a fee for incoming telegraphic transfers and then refuse to let the depositor write checks on these funds for several days are essentially doing the same.

Think about it. If you pay a trusted individual to take a negotiable instrument to your bank and deposit it in your account, but that individual instead puts the funds into his or her own interest-bearing account for a few days, and keeps the interest, and does this without your permission, then you should have the right to seek compensation in the courts. Some banks do this every day and get by with it. They know that it will be difficult, at best, for the individual to obtain the evidence needed to substantiate charges and that the cost of legal fees will likely far outweigh the compensation to be derived.

Delays in transfers are not only limited to small amounts. For example, a $1,500,000 transfer intended to go to the manufacturer of equipment was "lost" in the system for over a month. The interest rate in the short-term money market at the time was 11%. Therefore, the bank(s) had the opportunity to make approximately $13,750 at the expense of the vendor of the goods.

There was a domino effect to this particular transaction because the goods were going to be shipped to a foreign customer and had to be loaded on a specific ship on a specific date in order to arrive at the scheduled time for incorporation into the project. The commercial terms between buyer and seller required the funds to be in a neutral account prior to the equipment being loaded on the ship. Since the funds didn't arrive as scheduled, the ship departed without the equipment. Using the best alternate shipping available, the equipment eventually reached its destination some 60 days late. This resulted in an equal delay for the entire project.

Other Reasons for Delays in the Transfer of Funds

Unfortunately, there is also the possibility that the transfer of funds might be delayed by persons in the employer's Finance or Accounting

Departments. Assume that the employee has received monthly paid funds on time for several months. Then suddenly the funds are arriving late by 15 days. The employee goes to the senior person in the Finance and Accounting Department and asks that the transfer be traced to find out what has happened. The payroll clerk brings the records and the employee is shown the instruction to the employer's bank which made the transfer at the usual time, just as in previous months. Eventually, the funds do arrive in the employee's account. However, similar delays occur several times in succeeding months. The appearance is that the banks are delaying the transfer.

This is not necessarily so. That is only one of several possibilities. Another possibility is that the company simply doesn't have the funds available to pay the employee and is too embarrassed to admit it. As previously mentioned, "Face" is all important in developing countries. The transfer instructions are, indeed, prepared and sent to the bank. The employer can show this to the employee to prove that they have done their part. But what the employee is not told is that there is no money in the employer's account and that the bank will not process the transfer. Another possibility is that someone in the employer's Finance and Accounting Department has contacted the bank officer in charge of the employer's business and told him or her to hold the transfer instructions until instructed otherwise. Unless the employee has a friend at the same bank who has access to the transfer records, there is no way to find out what really happened.

Another possibility is that someone in the employer's Finance Department, perhaps with instructions from or the approval of others, put the funds temporarily into his own interest-bearing account. The employer may have an employee payroll of hundreds of thousands of dollars per month if he is, for example, a large contractor working on several major projects. If there is a relative or friend with the employer's bank who has influence or control over telegraphic transfers, and is willing to cooperate, it is not too difficult to arrange such schemes in some countries.

One solution for the employee is to receive all compensation in traveler's checks or cash, go to the bank personally and deposit or transfer the funds as appropriate. However, this might be inconvenient in some locations as well as time consuming. Where cash is the only alternative there is also the question of security because it is generally unwise to carry large quantities, even for short trips such as from the office to the bank.

5

Attachment III: Insurance

The following is a summary of the types, amounts, and general terms of insurance that the employer shall provide employee, and covered dependents, during the term of the agreement:

1. Term life insurance

Employee shall be covered by the amount of $_____ employee's spouse by the amount of $_____, and each covered dependent, other than employee's spouse, by the amount of $_____. Details of the limits and exclusions of this coverage are contained in the policies issued by the insurance company. The name of the insurance company providing this coverage and the policy numbers are as follows:

(Here list the name of the insurance company, policy numbers and name of person to whom each applies.)

2. Accidental death and dismemberment insurance

Employee and covered dependent(s) shall be provided twenty-four (24)-hour coverage under this policy, throughout the life of the agreement, in the amount of $_____ for employee, $_____ for employee's spouse, and each covered dependent, other than employee's spouse, by the amount of $_____. Details of the limits and exclusions of this coverage are contained in the policies issued by the insurance company. The name of the insurance company providing this coverage and the policy numbers are as follows:

(Here list the name of the insurance company, policy numbers and name of person to whom each applies.)

3. Loss of income insurance

Employee shall be compensated by an amount equivalent to two-thirds employee's monthly base salary for every month employee is physically or mentally incapacitated for any reason whatever, other than a job-related incident, and unable to remain employed in the type of work in which employee is trained and experienced. Payments under this coverage shall begin on the first day of the sixth (6ᵗʰ) calendar month of such incapacitation. Details of the limits and exclusions of this coverage are contained in the policy issued by the insurance company. The name of the insurance company providing this coverage and the policy number are as follows:

(Here list the name of the insurance company and policy number.)

4. Workmen's compensation insurance

Employee shall be provided workmen's compensation insurance for any loss of income or incapacitation due to injuries sustained while on the job and employed under this agreement in an amount equal to a maximum benefit of seventy-two (72) months base salary. The name of the insurance company providing this coverage and the policy number are as follows:

(Here list the name of the insurance company and policy number.)

5. Personal effects insurance

Employee has been provided replacement cost coverage for the personal effects of employee and covered dependent(s). In general, this coverage includes, but is not limited to, fire, storm, theft, mysterious disappearance, water damage from any source, abandonment by employee or destruction as a result of military or police actions, civil unrest, riots, wars whether declared or undeclared, or any other or similar circumstances which may develop in the geographic area of the permanent residence place and that is beyond the control of employee. Such coverage has been arranged prior to the packing and shipping of employee's and covered dependent's personal effects from employee's point of origin. The name of the insurance company providing this coverage and the policy numbers are as follows:

(Here list the name of the insurance company and policy number.)

General Notes

- Proceeds, if any, that may come due under any or all of the above insurance shall be for the benefit of the employee, employee's covered dependent(s), or beneficiaries, as appropriate. In no case shall proceeds be shared with the employer nor premiums deducted from any amount or amounts payable to employee or employee's beneficiary.

- All insurance benefits which may accrue under the agreement are *in addition* to any insurance employee may presently have as of the date of the Agreement, or which employee may obtain privately during the term of the agreement.

- All insurance shall be carried through internationally recognized insurance companies acceptable to both employer and employee.

- The insurance coverage listed in this attachment III is in effect concurrent with the date of the agreement. Concurrent with signing of the agreement, employer has handed over *original* copies of proof of coverage and proof of payment of the first years premiums. Hereafter, employer shall pay the premiums on or before the dates due so that there is no interruption in coverage throughout the life of the agreement.

- Insurance coverage provided under the agreement shall not be renegotiated with any agency or company, terminated and assigned to a new or alternate company, or in any other way modified without the prior written consent of employee. Employee shall have the right to communicate directly with any agency or company providing coverage under the agreement for the purpose of verifying that premiums have been paid and that coverage remains in effect. Should employer take any action whatever contrary to the terms of this paragraph, or fail to make premium payments on or before the dates due, such action or failure shall constitute a material breach of the agreement.

This attachment is a *guide* to the types of insurance that should be provided in the agreement. The limits of coverage and some of the verbiage will have to be modified to meet specific employee/employer situations. For example, the employer may already have insurance coverage for employees that varies from what is written here. Therefore, some negotiations may be necessary. If this is the case, then the employee should review all proposed policies with an insurance consultant before agreeing to them.

The suggested procedures for obtaining insurance coverage and being sure the policies remain in effect are spelled out in the attachment itself and need no further comment.

Workmen's Compensation for Household Staff

In addition to the insurance which applies to the employee and dependents directly, the employee should obtain workmen's compensation coverage for the household staff. In fact, this may be required by local law. The employer will provide this if the household staff are hired through him. Alternately, the employee will have to pay. In my experience the cost has been quite nominal.

Liability Insurance

The employee should obtain liability insurance to cover damages to the landlord's property or other incidents for which the employee or dependents could be held responsible.

Automobile Insurance

If the employee has automobile insurance in his country of origin he should check with his agent to see if he will be covered while operating a vehicle in the country to which he is moving. If not, he should obtain coverage before driving in that country.

Note that the terms of automobile insurance require that premium payments be made on the dates specified in the policy. Since the cost of such insurance is typically high in developing countries, the employer may apply for coverage, even be issued a statement by the insurance company indicating he is covered, but actually never pay the premium. When an incident occurs, the insurance company first deducts the outstanding premium; the remainder is used to pay the claim. If the insurance company balks at this arrangement, then the employer simply moves coverage to a different company.

Verification of Beneficiary

The employee should verify that the beneficiary named in the employment forms is the beneficiary named in the forms that are received and processed by the insurance company. The employee should do this personally through direct contact with the agent (or agents). The agent's confirmation should be in writing, not just verbal. The employee should preferably do this before moving to the new location.

This may seem an unusual precaution. However, it is not unheard of for the documents to be revised naming an alternate beneficiary so that any funds that become payable go to him first. He is then in a position to *bargain* with the employee (or the beneficiary intended by the employee) to reduce the amount received by the employee and pocket the remainder. At the very least, the benefits may be reduced by the amount of the premium if not paid. Therefore, the agent (or agents) should also be asked to verify that all premium payments have been made when due.

The employer, on his part, may empathize with the employee or the employee's intended beneficiary, but rationalize that the unfortunate incident has also hurt the employer's business economically and that he deserves some compensation as well. Perhaps the employee may not have been employed long enough to make a significant contribution to the employer's business; if the employee is incapacitated the employer will have to write off the cost of recruiting and relocating the employee and start again. In any case, any compensation the employer believes his company needs should come from a separate insurance policy, not the insurance intended for the employee or the employee's beneficiary. Although I know of an incident, I do not believe that this is a common practice. I offer these comments only as an indication of a potential difference in business practices with which an employee should be prepared to deal.

Finding Someone to Turn to in Case of Need

We would all prefer never to be involved in an incident that results in an insurance claim. However, life is not usually that simple. Any expatriate reading this who believes otherwise should not consider working in a developing country.

If an incident does occur, the expatriate (and dependents) may not be in condition to look after themselves or their personal property. Therefore, the expatriate should find someone in the local community, in addition to the employer, who can be trusted and who will agree to represent or assist the employee (or the beneficiary) in case of need. The expatriate should do this soon after arrival in the country of employment. The expatriate's instructions to this person should be in writing, registered, and otherwise comply with all local laws concerning such agreements. A statement should be included concerning limits of authority.

6

Attachment IV: Guide for Selecting Employee's Residence

Housing varies considerably in developing countries and from location to location within a given country—not unlike it does in developed countries. Therefore, the following must be used only as a guide for preparing a list of requirements tailored to a specific location. The facilities described represent, in general, the minimum acceptable standard for a residence in a tropical climate. There are some obvious changes that should be incorporated if the assignment is going to be in a colder climate—(e.g., no need for a swimming pool). The standards described here may be achieved by the selection of an existing residence that already meets these or greater standards, through renovation of an existing structure that can be made to comply with these standards, or by new construction.

1. General Notes

- All dimensions shown are in feet unless otherwise noted.
- Ceiling heights are to be eight (8) ft. or higher above floor level.
- Where practicable, each room should have at least one wall facing the garden. In tropical areas this wall should have floor to ceiling windows or sliding doors with substantial locks.
- The entire facility should be thoroughly washed down with a strong bleach/water solution to kill fungus and mildew before occupancy.
- All cracks, openings around windows, and similar defects should be caulked and painted. Colors to be chosen by employee.
- Where tile work is garish or not considered in good taste, in employee's sole opinion, it should be replaced by tile acceptable to employee.

- The house must not be located in a low area subject to flooding or that can be isolated by flooding of normal access roads or highways, in an area where mud slides could occur, or in similar bad locations. The house should not be near ponds, swamps, and streams or rivers unless specifically selected by employee. The property must be laid out and at such an elevation that rain run-off from neighboring property does not flow onto the property upon which employee's residence is situated.

- The main lower level of the house must be no less than two (2) ft. above street level.

- All floors should be constructed of concrete poured over a vapor barrier (or equivalent). Floors that do not have wall-to-wall carpet are to be parquet/wood upstairs, or marble or terrazzo downstairs (if a two-story house). Kitchens and baths to have tiled floors and walls up to wainscot level.

- The house must have a well-constructed and efficiently designed gutter and drainage system.

- There should not be any open sewers or cesspools. It is preferred that all street drains and sanitary sewers be covered and contained in underground systems.

- All streets and access roads associated with the residence or leading to it should be paved and suitable for travel in all weather.

- The house location should be analyzed for the time required to reach school, work, medical aid, shopping, the residences of other staff members or customer's staff with whom employee works and/or socializes, social clubs, golf course, etc.

- The employee should analyze the neighborhood with respect to ages of children and adults. Arrange through the agent or landlord to meet neighbors on all sides of a prospective house. Try to get an opinion from local police concerning security in the area and a list of any crime that has occurred in recent past.

- Grounds, plants, trees and shrubbery should be in good repair and well laid out with paved walks between modules, the swimming pool, garage, etc. (as appropriate to the facility).

2. Master Bedroom and Bath

The master bedroom should have an adjoining private, modern (U.S.-style) bathroom including tub with shower, toilet, two (2) built-in lavatories, large wall mirrors, built-in cabinets and linen storage shelves. Mirrors over lavatories must be well lighted, preferably surrounded by lights. Bedroom should be approximately 18 ft. × 20 ft., bath 9 ft. × 12 ft.

The master bedroom is to have a dressing area between the bedroom proper and the bathroom, which is additional to the space occupied by the bath and bedroom. This space is to contain at least 16 linear ft. of built-in closet and storage space that extends from floor to ceiling. Closets should have doors with locks and be no less than 2-ft. deep, inside dimension from front to back.

3. Additional Bedrooms and Baths

One additional bedroom for each covered dependent but in no case less than two (2) such bedrooms. A shared bathroom equivalent to the master bath is acceptable for each two bedrooms. Each bedroom to be approximately 14 ft. × 16 ft. All bedrooms to have at least 12 ft. of built-in closet/storage area in each room. Closets to have doors with locks and be no less than 2 ft. deep, inside dimension from front to back.

4. Study or Office

The study or office should be approximately 16 ft. × 20 ft. It should have one combination bookcase/base cabinet unit 8 feet long.

5. Television and Recreation Room

A separate room to be furnished for television, video, audio, and general recreation. This room is to be isolated from the main living area. Approximate size to be 14 ft. × 16 ft. The room is to contain one combination bookcase, television, video, and stereo system cabinet approximately 12 ft. long with base storage unit.

6. Living Room

The approximate size of the living room is to be 24 ft. × 30 ft. It is preferable that at least one wall face the garden and be comprised entirely of floor to ceiling windows and/or sliding doors.

7. Dining Room

The dining room should be approximately 14 ft. × 18 ft.

8. Kitchens

In tropical areas it is common to have separate *wet* and *dry* kitchens. Cleaning of vegetables, washing of dishes, and similar wet tasks are done in the wet kitchen; cooking and final meal preparation are done in the dry kitchen. Both wet and dry kitchens should have approximately 18 linear ft. of counter 2 ft. wide with base cabinets below and wall cabinets above. There should be a pass-through counter/window between kitchens. Each kitchen should be approximately 14 ft. × 16 ft.

Each kitchen should have a double sink, with each compartment of each sink approximately 16 in. sq. Each sink should be served by a hot-and-cold water mixer faucet and with a separate retractable spray or rinsing hose.

9. Pantry

The pantry should be equipped with storage shelves floor to ceiling on at least two walls. It should be located adjacent to the dry kitchen and be easily accessed from the service entrance. The pantry should be approximately 8 ft. × 12 ft.

10. Laundry

The laundry room should be adjacent to the pantry and kitchens. The laundry should contain connections for washer, dryer, and ironing. There should be space for a 3 ft. × 4 ft. work table and for an ironing board. Overall, the laundry should be approximately 12 ft. × 16 ft., well lighted and ventilated. An exhaust fan in the ceiling or a window is recommended.

11. Kitchen and Laundry Appliances and Cabinets

The kitchen is to be provided with a gas range and oven and a microwave type oven. Many developing nations have minimal natural gas distribution grids and rely more on bottled LP-gas (propane). Gas range to be of large size with four burners and a separate grill on top, oven approximately 24 inches wide, 18 in. high, and 18 in. deep, with broiler below. The microwave oven to have inside dimensions of approximately 20 in. wide, 15 in. high, and 15 in. deep. A large vent hood is to be provided over the range that exhausts to the outside of the house.

There should be two (2) refrigerators of approximately 34 cu. feet capacity each and each with ice-making capability, one (1) chest type freezer of at least 30 cu. feet capacity, one (1) automatic washing machine of minimum 15 lbs. capacity, and a matching dryer.

12. Staff Accommodations

Staff accommodations should be clean, well ventilated, individual rooms for each staff member except married couples need only one room. Each room should be approximately 10 ft. × 12 ft. Accommodations should be furnished for at least the chief cook, gardener, house boy, and two (2) maids. Staff facilities should include communal facilities including at least one (1) bathroom with shower, toilet, and lavatory; separate cooking facilities with stove, oven, and small refrigerator; and a sitting or lounge area. One moderate size storage room should be provided for staff for storage of personal effects and food. Facilities must be sunlit at least part of the day, preferably all day.

13. Garage

The residence should have a two-car garage. The garage should have a sturdy steel door or doors. There should be a separate passage door. The garage size should be approximately 24 ft. × 26 ft. (inside dimensions).

14. Store Room

There should be a store room near the garage, approximately 10 ft. × 12 ft. and fitted out complete with shelves and lighting. This room is to have a heavy-duty door with stout hinges and lock. It is to be well ventilated and in a dry location.

15. Doors, General

All doors, both inside and to exterior, must be provided with robust locks and hinges. Locks must be of high quality. Locks should be of the dead-bolt type with a bolt no less than 1 in. in diameter, and it should penetrate the matching door or frame no less than 1 in. All locks should be of the same brand. If the house is not new, then all locks shall be reset by a recognized, bonded locksmith. Keys should be handed over to employee arranged on a master key ring and have one complete duplicate set. No other party shall be allowed to keep keys for the residence of employee. In addition, all exterior doors should have sliding bolts at top and bottom that pin into the concrete floor or the frame over the door.

Each door shall have no less than three (3) hinges. Doors shall be set and hinges arranged so that the hinge pins can only be removed from inside the space served.

16. Window Screens

All windows should be provided with insect screens. There should be screen doors at the outside entrance to the kitchen/pantry/laundry areas and at the front door at discretion of the employee.

17. Curtains and Drapes

There should be valances above all windows with dual tracks for drapes and sheer curtains. All drapes and curtains should be selected by the employee. Drapery material is to be heavy-duty and provided with sound-deadening liner. Drapes and curtains should be provided and installed so that light cannot penetrate from either direction, day or night.

18. Burglar Bars

Burglars bars should be provided for all windows, over skylights, and light wells. Burglar bars over windows should be provided with release mechanisms from inside the room served.

19. Carpets

There should be wall-to-wall carpet with under pad in bedrooms, study, and television rooms. Quality and color should be selected by the employee from locally available stock.

20. Furniture

All furniture should be quality wood and fabric, and the colors should be selected by employee. Furniture should include (but is not limited to): king-sized bed with box springs and foam mattress, couch, chairs, bureau, wall mirrors, end tables and lamps for master bed-room, similar furnishings for each additional bed room except beds will be chosen appropriate to the person occupying the room), dining room table and eight chairs, sideboard for dining room, couch, chairs, tables, lamps, etc. appropriate in size and number to size and arrangement of living room, 4 ft. round table with four chairs in kitchen, bed, table and chair in each staff room, dining table, chairs, lounge furniture in staff living area, stove and miscellaneous cooking utensils for staff kitchen, outdoor type tables, chairs and lounge furniture appropriate to the pool patio area, miscellaneous lamps, mirrors, pictures and similar items that are appropriate to the facilities. The exact details of items to be furnished by the employer should depend on the quantity of furnishings in employee's personal effects being shipped to the permanent residence place and the house finally selected by employee.

21. Perimeter Wall and Exterior Security

The residence should be surrounded by a stoutly built, 14 ft. high (minimum) concrete or brick wall with a barbed wire fence built above the wall on 3 ft. high "Y" posts spaced no more than 5 ft. apart. There should be an electrically charged wire set in the crotch of the "Y" on insulators. It is advisable to place *Concertina wire* in the crotch of the "Y". There should be sturdy steel gates, minimum of seven (7) ft. high, at each entrance. Gates should open by sliding rather than swinging open on hinges. Gates should have robust, double bar-type locks that fix the gates at both top and bottom. All roof, wall, and other areas accessible from adjacent property or structures should be protected by barbed wire, steel grates, and electric fence. Decorative steel security grille should be provided over windows, skylights, and so forth.

22. The Roof

The roof must be in excellent repair, with no signs of leaks either in the attic or on the ceiling below. Since it is possible to hide previous leakage problems by paint, the employer must guarantee that the roof will not leak and be willing to repair any leaks immediately that do occur and to replace any damaged carpets, drapes, or other furnishings at employer's cost. The roof should be constructed so that burglars cannot enter through vents or by simply lifting up the roof tiles (where that type of roof is used).

23. Telephone System

The house is to be served by a Touch-Tone, international direct dial telephone system with phones in master bedroom, study or office, TV and audio room, living room, kitchen, and one other bedroom (to be selected). Two (2) private telephone lines should serve the house. All telephones should be equipped to receive or send on either line and should include a "hold" feature. Telephones should be portable with 12 ft. extension cords and snap-in wall jacks. Employer is to provide all licenses required for the operation/use of telephones, television and radio receivers, and videos at no cost to employee.

24. Intercom System

The house is to be equipped with an intercom system connecting the master bedroom, study/office, kitchen, and security guard's normal duty station. The master station should be in the master bedroom.

25. Security Alarm System

An alarm should be built into the electric fence control that sets off if fence grounded. Visual and audible alarm indicators should be in the master bedroom, guard's normal duty station, kitchen, and study/office.

26. Electrical System, General

The electrical system serving the house and attached facilities must be designed and installed professionally, in good repair, with receptacles and fixtures grounded throughout through specially installed copper ground rods no less than 1/2 in. in diameter and driven 6 ft. into the ground. Under no circumstances shall any electrical circuit be grounded to water or gas pipes. Receptacles must be of the type that will accept a grounded plug/appliance.

The main panel must be capable of handling the full night-time load (all air conditioners, lights, pumps and similar) but in no case of less than 23,000 watts connected capacity. The main panel should be supplied by public power through a full-capacity voltage regulator and, alternately, a 6,000-watt standby generator. This capability is to be accomplished through a separate interlock type switch panel that will only allow power to be supplied from one or the other systems to the main panel. The main panel should be supplied with sufficient circuit breakers so that when the standby generator is used only one wall receptacle in each room can be selected to receive power (for lighting), all ceiling fans can be operated, power supplied to the refrigerators and freezer and to the pool pump. These consumers will be served by turning off all circuit breakers and selecting only those that are essential at the moment and within the 6,000-watt generator capability.

The standby generator should be mounted in a separate room that is designed and built for maximum security against theft. The room must be well ventilated. The generator should be a name brand and be complete with electric starter, self-contained control panel, low oil level warning/cutout device, self-contained fuel tank and dual voltage (115/220). The generator should be mounted off the floor with no less than 2 ft. of walkway all around or as additionally required for ease of maintenance. The generator should be connected electrically to a breaker box mounted on the inside wall of the generator room which, in turn, should be connected to the interlock switch panel. The electric starter should be supplied power from a heavy-duty, truck-type battery also mounted inside the generator room. The battery should be kept charged by a trickle charger, which receives its power from the house main panel and is disconnected from the main panel when the interlock switch is set to supply power from the standby generator.

27. Lighting, General

All lighting should be tested in the presence of employee to ensure adequacy. For example, kitchens should have bright, general lighting, and additional fluorescent light fixtures under cabinets above counters; the study/office should also be brightly lit. All lavatories should be especially well lit.

28. Exterior Floodlighting

There should be floodlights around exterior of the house up under the eaves, around any inside gardens or light wells, and at strategic locations around the perimeter fence and about the grounds surrounding the house. All such security lighting should be sufficient in number and intensity to easily recognize any person or animal that may enter the premises. Shrubbery should be back-lighted to reduce the probability of persons or animals hiding in such locations. All security lighting should be controlled from a switch in the master bedroom and one other location selected by employee.

29. Air-Conditioning

Air-conditioning should be available in each room throughout house. Capacity of each unit must be suitable to maintain an inside temperature of maximum 80° F with an outside temperature of 105° F. In addition, each room should be served by no less than one or more ceiling fans, each with blade diameter of no less than 54 in. and multiple-speed controls. Each air conditioner and fan should be controlled from individual wall-mounted controls in the room served.

All air-conditioning units inside the residence must be very quiet when operating. The employee should be able to carry on a normal conversation in any room with all air conditioners operating at maximum capacity. Each air-handling unit must have a filter system that can be removed, cleaned, and reused. (Note that the term *air-conditioning* includes both heating and cooling. However, it is recognized that *heating* may not be required in tropical climates unless the residence is at a higher elevation.) All air conditioners and duct work should be *thoroughly cleaned* of fungus and other growth that could cause respiratory irritation or diseases.

30. Water System

There should be a municipal and private potable water supply, each of which can be individually selected through a manifold, supplying water to an elevated tank of at least 2,000 liter capacity. The storage tank should have a screened vent. The minimum head at any discharge point to be 16 ft. (gravity flow from the tank). Incoming water should be processed through one of two replaceable cartridge-type filters (make AMF) prior to discharge into the storage tank. These filters should be manifolded so that one can remain in service while the other is being serviced. The water level in the tank should be controlled by float valve. Discharge from the tank should be selective by way of a manifold from which water can be directed to a pressure pump or directly to the facilities by gravity flow in case of electrical failure. Pressure pump should be provided with a 200 liter vertical pressure tank. Minimum/maximum pressures to be 35/45 psig. Discharge water should pass through a dual filter manifold identical to incoming water filters, and a quality water softener. In addition, all water should be processed through an ultraviolet, anti-bacterial device made by a recognized international firm and installed and maintained by the firm's authorized representative. At no time should the bacteria count in water taken from any discharge point in the house be greater than 35 parts per million (ppm).

The private water system should consist of an electric-driven, deep well pump that is supplied from an aquifer containing clear, clean, cool, potable water that is frequently tested by a recognized authority acceptable to the employee. The private system should be manifolded so that it can provide water in case of failure of the municipal system. The employer should provide all replacement filters and regular recharging of the water softener.

Distribution piping should be minimum 1 in. plastic (or copper). It should be demonstrated that any shower can be used without appreciable reduction in the water being supplied to it when any near or remote toilet is flushed, when faucets are used in the kitchen, or when the clothes washer is used.

31. Hot Water System

The house must have a hot water system for baths and kitchens. It is preferred that each bath and kitchen have separate electric or gas hot water heaters rather than one central unit. Solar heating of water is also preferred as a supplement to the electric or gas systems. The temperature of water delivered from each heater should be controllable. Hot water at up to 180° F should be available in each kitchen.

32. Sanitary Sewer and Drains

The sewer system must be designed and installed professionally and totally enclosed. All drains—including those in floors as well as at fixtures—should have traps that prevent sewer gas from entering the house and must be connected to a vent stack that extends above the roof of the house. All drains should have removable grills or screens covering the opening. Where any sewer or storm water drain discharges into a public ditch or similar collection system, the discharge end should be covered with a screen mesh of approximately 0.5×0.5 in. pattern and well secured in place to prevent snakes and rodents from entering the premises through the drains.

33. Swimming Pool

There should be a swimming pool approximately 18 ft. $\times$ 36 ft. inside dimensions and no less than 8 ft. deep at the deep end and 4 ft. deep at the shallow end. The pool should include a skimmer system with no less than two skimmers and a drain at the lowest point; these should be connected to a manifold or selector valve on the suction side of a circulating pump. The circulating pump should be at least 2 1/2 H.P. and equipped with a basket-type strainer. There should be a diatomaceous earth filter system. There should be at least four return jets, but in any case there should be enough to ensure continuous circulation throughout pool. The pool should be surrounded by a sun deck with a nonskid surface. There should be an adjacent patio approximately 14 ft. $\times$ 20 ft. suitable for deck chairs, tables, and an outdoor grill.

34. Swimming Pool Bath and Toilet

A separate bath house and toilet near the swimming pool are preferred rather than having to use the facilities within the house.

35. Pest Control

The house should be thoroughly fumigated, checked for termites, rats, bats, and other pests prior to occupancy. Employer shall provide the services of a licensed, professional pest control company to spray or otherwise control insects both inside and on the grounds surrounding the house. This service should include fogging nearby foliage, sumps, ponds, ditches and so forth, which may be located outside the premises, to eliminate mosquitoes. Pest control services should be provided at least once each month. The employee should receive a written description of the chemicals and/or other products used and should have the right to stop the use of any or all chemicals and products at employee's sole discretion. If the pest control company cannot furnish an acceptable replacement, then the employer should not have any further responsibility for providing pest control at the employee's residence.

7

Attachment V: Employee's Job Description

The following format is a guide to use in preparing employee job descriptions. Data entered should be specific, stated clearly, and well defined. Diction should be carefully chosen. Each job description should be prepared in relation to all other job descriptions. Job descriptions should be carefully analyzed during their preparation to insure that duplication of function does not occur. Where overlap or coordination is necessary, additional clarification should be provided.

Employee's Title or Position

The employee's title should be shown on a company organization chart. The chart should be dated and approved by the employer's chief executive officer. A copy should be attached to the job description.

Department, Subsidiary, or Organization to Which Employee Is Assigned

Self-explanatory. Should be on the same chart.

Executive Memo Authorizing Position

It is usual practice that the chief executive officer has the final approval of all positions as well as the hiring and number of personnel in each department and the company as a whole. When a department recognizes a need for additional employees, a memo justifying the need and recommending the action to be taken is prepared by the department head. He then passes this memo, with supporting documentation as necessary, up the chain of command. If acceptable to intermediate levels of authority, it eventually reaches the chief executive officer. The chief executive officer approves, disapproves, or sends it back for modification. The hiring of an expatriate is usually a decision emanating from the company executive level, and the decision-making process will likely involve the chief executive officer from the start. In any case, there is normally an executive memo issued authorizing the effort required to find and hire the employee. A copy of this is usually sent to the chief financial officer for his records. A copy of this memo should be attached to the employee's job description. If the memo has a *reference number* it should be entered here.

Date of Executive Memo

This is the date of the executive memorandum.

Name and Title of Person Employee Reports To

Self-explanatory. Should be the next higher level of authority shown on the organization chart. However, this should not be assumed. Write it down.

Employee's Required Background

Each of the following should be described in enough detail to make clear what "Body of Knowledge" the person in this position must have to be able to meet the employer's requirements:

- Formal education
- Special schools or training
- Languages
- Leadership ability and personality
- Number of years in industry
- Number of years in similar assignment
- Field experience
- Office experience
- Total working years
- Administrative ability
- Organizational ability
- Sales ability
- Foreign experience
- References

Employee's Authority

Provide a description of the authority, actions, and level of decision making that will be assigned to the employee. The following can be used as a guide:

- Provide decision-making diagrams that describe how decisions at different levels of authority within the company are made.

- Provide an organigram showing the staff positions that will be under the employee's direct supervision.

- Describe the employee's authority and the process by which subordinate positions will be filled.

- Describe the employee's authority and the process by which subordinates may be terminated.

- Describe the employee's authority and the process by which the number of subordinates supervised may be increased or decreased.

- Describe the facilities and equipment that will be under the direct control of the employee and the process by which adjustments increasing or decreasing this allowance will be made. Be specific, identify offices, number of desks, computers, file cabinets, telephones, facsimile and photocopy machines, and so forth. Where a specific type is required provide that information.

- Describe the process by which the facilities and equipment under the direct control of the employee will be obtained and the employee's authority to select/purchase these. If already in existence, identify/describe.

- Describe the process by which facilities and equipment under the direct control of the employee will be maintained and the employee's authority to order maintenance services.

- Prepare detailed codes of accounts for all overhead items as well as the projects or other work assigned to the employee. The employer and employee should determine/agree jointly on the monthly and annual budget for each item in the code of accounts.

- Prepare a statement that explains how budget variances, if any, will be handled.

- Prepare an explanation of interfacing relations with:
  —Customers
  —Company executives
  —Other department heads and personnel

Limits of Authority

Limits of signature authority should be established for the following:

Departmental Purchase Orders

Purchase orders for administrative support equipment, supplies, and other administrative needs (such as consultants) *within* the department in which the employee works, and the maximum monetary limit of any individual purchase order.

Company Administrative Support Purchase Orders

Purchase orders for administrative support equipment, supplies, and other administrative needs *for the company* and the maximum monetary limit of any individual purchase order.

Monetary Limit for Revenue Jobs

The maximum monetary limit for any one purchase for any single revenue-producing project.

Monetary Limit for Capital Equipment

The maximum monetary limit for any one capital equipment or parts replacement purchase for company-owned facilities or equipment.

Annual Budget for Department or Assignment

State the annual budget for each department or project to which the employee is assigned and the total. Detail how cost information will be gathered and the schedule for periodic review. The employee should have access to all backup data used to report costs for which employee is responsible, and the time and staff to review these costs *prior to* any report of these costs to management.

Monetary Limit for Business Entertainment

Maximum limit of business entertainment expense for any one encounter and maximum overall average per month. (*Note*: this refers to entertainment only and not total expenses.)

Overlapping and Coordinating Functions

Description of employee's areas of authority that may overlap with the authority of other classifications. Describe how such overlap will be handled in the day-to-day routine. Describe all coordinating relationships. Provide a chart that shows these relationships and attach it to the job description.

Schedule for Employment

A schedule should be prepared that describes the time from the decision to hire a new employee until that person is in place and meeting or exceeding the employer's expectations. Typical tasks appearing in this schedule would be similar to the following ones. The time reference is to the *employee's* time (the labor hours) required to complete each task. Specific assignments may require additional tasks to those shown below. Also, the tasks shown below may not be in the order in which they occur:

- Date of hire—a milestone
- Time required to process work permits, visas, etc.
- Time required to pack personal effects and arrange shipping
- Time en route
- Date of arrival—a milestone
- First date in office—a milestone
- Time required to process through national and local authorities
- Time required to set up employee's payroll information
- Time required to interview prospective staff and hire
- Time required to set up office, assuming that office space is already available and adequate:
  —Prepare list of requirements and requisitions
  —Locate, purchase, and install furniture
  —Locate, purchase, and install office equipment
  —Order and install telephone and intercom system
  —Complete any other facility improvements necessary
- Time required to set up correspondence systems
- Time required to set up office accounting systems

- Time required to find permanent housing
- Time required to move into permanent housing
- Time required to meet key business associates
- Date by which employee is to meet or exceed the employer's expectations—a milestone

Review of Employee's Performance

The employee and his or her supervisor should meet and review the employee's performance on a periodic basis. The first review should be within three months of the employee reporting to work. Thereafter, a review every six months should be adequate. A good measure of performance is through feedback from the employee's customers. If the feedback is positive, and the employer's goals are being achieved on time and on budget, then it is likely that the employee is a positive asset to the company.

Schedule of Base Pay, Bonus, and Conditions Reviews

Base pay and bonus reviews are normally conducted at the same time as the employee's performance review. There should be a written agreement that spells out employee achievements that warrant increases in base pay or bonuses. In any case, there should be adjustments in base pay for changes in the cost of living. This should be based on a survey conducted by a third-party consultant. There are several companies that provide this service. The employee should consult with his or her accountant or embassy, either of which should be able to provide names of such companies conducting cost-of-living surveys in the area.

Miscellaneous

Documentation of the employee's job description, an understanding of the employer's management method and structure and organization are important for the previous reasons. It is also important that the employee and employer agree on the number and level of competence of the staff needed to support those activities for which employee will be responsible.

This staff may be many or few, depending on the nature of the assignment. In any case, this staff will probably consist of no less than a secretary or administrative assistant. Although this person can be considered as simply one of the resources that must be available to the employee, the secretary is perhaps the most vital communications link that the employee will have with persons both inside and outside the company. Because of this particular importance and the fact that really good secretaries are not easily found, it is important that the requirements of this position are understood and agreed to by both employee and the employer. For this reason, the outline in attachment VI is provided to use as a guide in screening secretarial applicants. (*Note*: secretaries may be male or female.)

8

Attachment VI: General Requirements for Secretaries

Typing Speed

Typing speed on IBM Selectric, PC, (or equal) should be 110 words per minute or better (in English). No mistakes. This must be done from new, unfamiliar (but clear), and handwritten script.

Knowledge of Computers

Must have a good general knowledge of computers and their operating systems. Experience in PC-type equipment is preferred. Must be able to install programs on both diskettes and hard disks.

Word Processing Experience

At the time this book was originally started (1987), the most popular word processing program in developing countries was WordStar.™ Programs come and go but, in any case, the employee may find that his or her favorite word processing program is little known or unknown in the country. This creates a dilemma. The program can be imported and the secretary trained. On the other hand, local support for the inevitable bugs may not be available, nor will there be other secretaries in the company to help when there is an overload, or when the secretary goes on vacation or is otherwise absent.

Any secretary who knows WordStar™ well can easily learn to use other programs. Therefore, if it proves difficult to impossible to find a secretary who has experience with the employee's favorite program, finding someone who knows WordStar™ and providing adequate training in the "new" software should not be difficult.

In any case, the secretary must be able to utilize all aspects of the word processing program. This includes enhanced features such as merge documents, headers and footers, multiple tabulations and column formatting, preparation of indexes, tables of contents, dot commands (in WordStar™), special printing features, and be generally at ease and familiar with the entire program.

Data Base Experience

Must be able to take rough idea or sketch and set up data base format, enter, index, sort, retrieve data, print out selected files and records; prepare and edit selected data for utilization with merge documents, print out reports and lists. Again, must generally be at ease and familiar with data base concept, and how it works with other programs.

Spread Sheet Program Experience

Must be able to use Lotus 1,2,3™ (or equivalent). Must be able to develop smooth report from supervisor's sketch. Should have a strong working knowledge of Lotus™ features, be able to edit formulas and make corrections approved by supervisor.

Knowledge of Employer's Business

Must be capable of learning and understanding the basic concepts around which the employer's business revolves. May be required to understand simple sketches and engineering drawings. Must have ability to visualize physical concepts. This does not mean that the candidate must have specific technical training. On the other hand, a lack of very basic ability in this area would make the job at times difficult to impossible. For example, without such ability it would be impossible to edit technical reports effectively for other than spelling, format, and punctuation. Some training may be required.

Knowledge of Filing Systems

Able to understand and maintain filing systems; must keep files and file index up-to-date without being reminded; keep track of files, who has them, and so forth. Periodically go through files to ensure all are in their proper places. With approval of supervisor, clean out and destroy old files no longer required, keep running list of such files.

Training Ability

Capable of personally supervising own training and training of less-experienced clerical staff in all skills areas.

Dictation

Able to take dictation in English at 120 words per minute or better. Must have experience with dictating machines, able to take cassette, transcribe, and type directly on typewriter or word processor.

Operation of Office Equipment

Must have the ability to read, understand, and carry out instructions pertaining to operation of all office equipment such as printers, telex, facsimile, telephone answering systems, typewriters, and photocopy machines, and so forth.

Knowledge of Telex and Facsimile Operations

Must have experience at sending and receiving domestic and international telexes and facsimiles.

Knowledge of Written and Spoken English

Able to easily communicate in written and spoken English and native language(s). Must be an excellent speller in both languages. Must have experience in the entire process of preparing manuscripts, studies, and so forth for publication and be able to prepare a company style manual, if it does not already exist.

Knowledge of Local History and Customs

Must have excellent knowledge of local history, customs, people, habits and protocol; and general knowledge of world history and politics.

Maintenance of Directories

Maintain orderly, up-to-date list of names, telephone, telex, and facsimile numbers, and addresses (etc.) of all persons, companies (etc.) with which the supervisor communicates, and in the form of a data base program.

Identification of Documents

Will see to it that every letter, telex, facsimile (etc.) has a job and file number in the heading or in the title block of drawings.

Control of Reports and other Documents

Must see that letters, memos, reports, and other documents are completed and arrive at their intended destination—on schedule. Will maintain separate logs of all incoming and outgoing correspondence including letters, memos, facsimiles, telex, and other documents.

Knowledge of Airline Reservation Systems

Must be familiar with the use of airline schedule tables for domestic and international routes, booking of air travel, hotel and rental car needs as required by the supervisor. Will keep a list of popular local restaurants, clubs, and similar places suitable for business entertainment.

Review and Preliminary Approval of Invoices

The secretary will review and preliminarily approve all invoices for telephone, telex, facsimile, temporary office help, office supplies, (etc.) that are being charged against the supervisor's activities. Keep a record of all such charges using spread sheet or data base programs. Periodically and routinely report weekly and monthly costs to the supervisor.

Personality and Appearance

Personality

Must be energetic, with outgoing personality and portray the concept of "sharpness" and good health.

Anticipation of Needs

Must quickly learn to anticipate needs. Must be an extension of the person to whom assigned; to be able to see as if through his or her eyes.

When Using the Telephone

Will often, probably several times each day, be required to make and receive calls to or from important customers, suppliers, subcontractors (etc.). Must be able to gracefully, and with wisdom, handle difficult communications situations. Must, on own initiative, know the whereabouts of all supervisors and staff and how each can be reached rapidly, and establish a system with other secretarial staff to carry this out.

Identification of Important Persons

Must be able to rapidly learn to identify the voices of persons who telephone or are called regularly, especially senior company staff and customers.

Resourcefulness

Must be resourceful. When information is needed, such as the location of a person who needs to be contacted, the secretary must persevere until the task is accomplished. He or she must make others within (and outside the company) who are assigned or associated with a task, aware of exactly what is to be done, who is going to be involved, what other resources are needed, who is going to be informed, and what time frame is allowed. In so many words, "The secretary must not give up just because a task appears difficult." The secretary must use reasonable judgment and move toward accomplishing a task in a professional manner. If not sure, the secretary must always ask for clarification and must never "assume." The secretary must understand the need to communicate or provide constant and reliable feedback to those who depend on information he or she is assigned to gather.

Dress and Habits

Must be orderly and neat in dress and habits. Style of attire must be business/executive oriented; makeup, if a female and if used, should not be glaring or ostentatious. In addition, the person should not be a smoker.

Working Hours

Must arrive for work on or before scheduled time. May be required to work after hours and weekends occasionally. Tardiness will not be tolerated nor long lunches or extended periods when no one knows the secretary's whereabouts. Always see to it that someone is alert to answer the telephone immediately throughout workday.

Other Requirements

Although the above may seem difficult and structured, the right person will understand and readily accept the self-discipline required to meet these requirements. This outline only typifies the requirements of a contemporary well-run company.

At the same time, the secretary will realize that neither he or she nor those with whom the secretary works will not make errors. The secretary will not dwell on his or her errors or those of others, but learn from these experiences and concentrate on positive factors. The secretary will have the quality of maintaining his or her own individuality and personality within a team relationship. The secretary must be loyal to his or her immediate supervisor and to the employer and have the good sense to understand and respect these relationships.

Required Background

Education

Graduated from senior high school and recognized secretarial college (at least two-year course) as a minimum; a degree from an accredited business administration course is desirable. An understanding of fundamental bookkeeping principles is required.

Minimum Experience Requirement

Must have at least five years administrative experience, preferably in (name type of company). Must have worked as an executive secretary for not less than two years.

Foreign Experience Requirement

Foreign experience in a similar field would be an advantage.

Specific Authority

Ordering of Departmental Materials

Order all materials normally required to support the work of the department.

Utilization of Company Facilities and Equipment

Utilize all company facilities and usual resources required in carrying out assigned work.

Control of Access to Department

Restrict entry of anyone to the facilities under the secretary's care; this includes the supervisor's office and desk, company and private files and bookcases, unless such person or persons have been authorized specific access in writing by the supervisor.

9

Evaluation of Terms
and Conditions

Both the employer and employee need to make a thorough evaluation of the prospective position or job. The employer needs to know beforehand if what will be offered is reasonable in comparison to the terms and conditions offered by other companies in the same or a similar business. The employee needs to evaluate each job offer to determine which proposal best meets his or her expectations. For such an evaluation to be meaningful, it should be done in a consistent format. Even if the employee has only one job offer, it should be analyzed in the same way to ensure that accepting it (or rejecting it) is not merely an emotional reaction.

The employer should note that this is *not* intended as a method of evaluating the employee's performance. Rather, it is a method of evaluating the position or job that the employee will be expected to perform and especially the terms and conditions attached to that position or job. However, it is a method that can be used by the employee to determine if the employer's business philosophy and practices, as well as the terms and conditions offered, will meet expectations.

Following this introduction is a typical list of statements and questions that might be considered. This list is only an example and can be used as a guide for preparing one's own special list. The list presented here is divided into the following sections:

A. General considerations

B. The company's organization and personnel

C. Authority and responsibility

D. The company's profitability and market forecast

E. Finance, accounting, and purchasing

F. Legal considerations

G.   Safety and security

H.   The compensation package offered

Each section is comprised of a number of individual statements and questions. Some are broken down into additional statements and questions. The special circumstances of a given employer/employee situation may require additional sections and questions that should be considered. These can easily be added to the list provided here with a word processing program (or, this list can be revised).

To the right of each statement or question are three columns. These are used by the employer (utilizing a scoring system) to determine how competitive the employer's offer is compared to other companies in the same or a similar business. This same method can be used by the employee to determine how well what is being offered meets the employee's expectations and needs.

In the list, the first column to the right is used to assign relative weights to each section. It is also used to assign relative weight to each statement and questions in each section. This is accomplished by first giving each section an overall relative weight that indicates the perception of its importance to each other section. The relative weight of each section is then distributed to the statements and questions in each section according to the perception of each statement's and the question's importance in relation to all other statements and questions in that section.

The scale of relative weights is typically a decimal number between .000 and 1.000. Each section, then, will have a decimal value of less than 1.000, for example .250; a question within this same section might have a relative weight of .015. The relative weights of all questions within a section must add up to the relative weight assigned to that section. The relative weight column of the entire list should add up to 1.000 (if the method suggested above is used). The relative weight of each question is also sometimes referred to as the weight factor.

The second column to the right is used to score each question. The *score* for each statement and question is based on the perception of how well the employer's proposal fits current standards or how well the employer's response meets the employee's expectations.

A scoring method must be used with which the employer (or employee) is comfortable. One method is to start with a generalized scale, (e.g., Poor, Acceptable, Good, and Better). Each of these, in turn, corresponds to a range of numbers on a numerical scale. Typically, the numerical scale might range from a low of zero (0) to a high of one hundred (100). "Poor" might correspond to the range zero (0) to twenty-five (25), "Acceptable" from twenty-six (26) to fifty (50), and so forth.

The *scores* for each item are multiplied by the relative weight of each item to arrive at an overall or adjusted score. This is entered in the third column to the right of the questions. The *adjusted scores* are then subtotaled for each section and totaled for the list. If the list is transferred to a spreadsheet program posting scores and modifications become easier.

The employer should prepare a copy of the list for each company to which the employer's company is being compared. Information about each company is gathered and scored, the scores analyzed, skewed responses eliminated, and a composite list of (what should be) acceptable terms and conditions prepared. If this process is done thoroughly and accurately, then the employer will know that the terms and conditions being offered are reasonable and fair.

The employee should prepare and score a list for each employer being considered. The adjusted scores of the lists are then compared to determine to give an indication of the (likely) order of choice.

Obviously, no such method, either the statements and questions or the scoring system, can avoid being subjective to a degree. Both the employer and employee need to do their homework and have a good idea of what terms and conditions are currently competitive. If one's homework is complete, then the statements and questions and responses expected should contain at least a shade of objectivity. The expectations of both parties establish the basis for negotiations. If the expectations of either are extreme, then reaching an amicable agreement will be difficult, perhaps impossible.

Job Conditions Evaluation Form

Date: _____

Company/Employer: _____

Employee's position or title: _____

A. General considerations

The first few are specifically for the employee and provide a quick indication of the need to continue discussions. There is little use in wasting either party's time if certain fundamentals are not acceptable:

Questions	Relative Weight	Score	Adjusted Weight
1. Will the work be fun?	____	____	____
2. Would I enjoy doing this every day?	____	____	____
3. Does my supervisor appear happy?	____	____	____
4. Does other management appear happy?	____	____	____
5. Do other employees appear happy?	____	____	____
6. Is work done in an atmosphere of seriousness or levity?	____	____	____
7. Does work appear to be a *team* effort?	____	____	____
8. Does the company regularly hold social functions such as parties, picnics, etc.?	____	____	____
9. Will I be able to use my best capabilities?	____	____	____
a. Organization and planning	____	____	____
b. Direct contact with key people	____	____	____
c. Overall supervision vs. details	____	____	____

    d. Participation in projects
       from start to finish   ____   ____   ____
    e. Participate in corporate
       planning   ____   ____   ____
    f. Others   ____   ____   ____

10. Do I have a sponsor and if so, is he or she in a high enough position to be effective?   ____   ____   ____

11. Will my spouse and children be happy with:
    a. The type of work I will be doing?   ____   ____   ____
    b. The company, its management, and other personnel?   ____   ____   ____
    c. The geographic area where we will have to live?   ____   ____   ____
    d. The climate?   ____   ____   ____
    e. Distance from friends and relatives?   ____   ____   ____
    f. Are there adequate schools within daily commuting distance or will children have to be taught at home or sent off to boarding school? ____   ____   ____
    g. The indigenous people in general?   ____   ____   ____

The following are applicable to both employer and employee:

12. Does the company use contemporary equipment such as computers, facsimile machines, and similar?   ____   ____   ____

13. If the answer to question 12 is yes, is this equipment up-to-date? ____   ____   ____

14. Are computers used by the majority of employees or just upper management secretaries?   ____   ____   ____

15. Is upper management computer literate?   ____   ____   ____

16. Are recent versions of software used?   ____   ____   ____

17. Is there an information systems supervisor or does every person have to solve his or her own computer problems? ____ ____ ____

18. Is there an efficient document control system? ____ ____ ____

19. Is there an efficient filing system? ____ ____ ____

20. Does the company maintain a technical library? ____ ____ ____

21. If there is a technical library, is someone assigned to control access and keep documents and files in order and up to date? ____ ____ ____

B. The company's organization and personnel

1. Is the organization well defined with charts, job descriptions, etc.? ____ ____ ____

2. Are the charts shown "real" or just for cosmetics? ____ ____ ____

3. Is the decision-making process obvious or obscure? ____ ____ ____

4. Are the persons who must carry out the company's objectives involved in the decision-making process? ____ ____ ____

5. If the answer to the above question is "yes," then is this involvement real or does management "massage" the employee's comments and suggestions to fit management's preconceived decisions? ____ ____ ____

6. Does success in the company depend on family relation, race, religious preference, school affiliation, nationality, or similar? ____ ____ ____

7. Are the age and training of management spread out over several people in different age groups so that if any one key person leaves or dies the company can continue to function uninterrupted? ___ ___ ___

8. What is the management turnover rate? ___ ___ ___

9. What is the turnover rate for other personnel? ___ ___ ___

10. What happened to the last person or persons who had the job now being offered? ___ ___ ___

11. What is the turnover rate in the job offered during the last five years? ___ ___ ___

12. Will the names and telephone numbers of the last two (three, four?) persons who held this job be given to the employee, if asked? ___ ___ ___

13. Can staff be expected to support the employee?
    a. Engineering ___ ___ ___
    b. Finance and Accounting ___ ___ ___
    c. Legal ___ ___ ___
    d. Purchasing ___ ___ ___
    e. Personnel ___ ___ ___
    f. Sales and Marketing ___ ___ ___
    g. Operations ___ ___ ___

14. Will the employee have the support of higher authority? ___ ___ ___

15. Is the company's relationship with employees good/ok/poor? ___ ___ ___

16. If a union company, is the relationship between the company and union good, ok, or poor? ___ ___ ___

17. If a union company, how does the union management feel about the company? ____ ____ ____

18. If a union company, is the existing contract long, medium, or short? ____ ____ ____

19. If a union company, how is the next union contract negotiation likely to impact the company's profits and future prospects? ____ ____ ____

20. If a union company, how many strikes, walkouts, or similar actions have occurred? ____ ____ ____

21. If strikes or walkouts occurred, was there any violence during the strike(s)? ____ ____ ____

22. Will the employee have to share secretarial support or will one be assigned directly to the employee? ____ ____ ____

23. What are the normal working hours? ____ ____ ____

24. How many hours per week will the employee have to work to accomplish assigned task? ____ ____ ____

25. Will work during the local two-day weekend normally be required?
    a. None ____ ____ ____
    b. One day? ____ ____ ____
    c. Both days? ____ ____ ____

26. If the answer to 25 is "yes," is compensatory time off given? ____ ____ ____

27. Do the company's *line* or *operations* functions have ultimate authority or do one or more *staff* functions control the company? ____ ____ ____

C. Authority and responsibility

1. To what extent are authority and responsibility delegated by upper management?   ____   ____   ____

2. Will the employee's immediate supervisor delegate authority *and* responsibility or just responsibility?   ____   ____   ____

3. Will the employee be able to choose/terminate those upon whom the employee's success relies, or is this subject to higher approval?   ____   ____   ____

4. Can the employee be ensured that sufficient authority will be delegated to manage assigned responsibilities?   ____   ____   ____

D. The company's profitability and market forecast

1. Has the company been profitable?   ____   ____   ____

2. Is the company profitable at present?   ____   ____   ____

3. Can it be expected to remain profitable?   ____   ____   ____

4. Has the company had steady growth?   ____   ____   ____

5. Have the ups and downs been mild or severe?   ____   ____   ____

6. What is the market forecast for the industry that the company is in?   ____   ____   ____

7. Does the company share its profits with employees in a logical and fair way?   ____   ____   ____

E. Finance, accounting, and purchasing

1. Does the company have a well
    thought out code of accounts and
    cost accounting system appro-
    priate to the type of business the
    company is in?   ____   ____   ____

2. Does the company have the cash
    (or outside) backing needed to
    support existing activities and
    future growth?   ____   ____   ____

3. Does the company routinely take
    advantage of discounts offered
    by vendors?   ____   ____   ____

4. Is the approval process for
    purchase orders efficient/fast
    or tedious/protracted?   ____   ____   ____

5. Does purchasing obtain
    permission before substituting
    items on a requisition or do
    they take unilateral action
    (no feedback)?   ____   ____   ____

6. Will the employee have control
    over all costs charged to
    assigned areas of responsibility?   ____   ____   ____

7. Will the employee have the
    authority to approve or
    disapprove all charges or
    invoices to assigned areas of
    responsibility?   ____   ____   ____

8. Are the company's rules and
    guidelines for company related
    expenses clear and fair?   ____   ____   ____

9. Does the company provide
    expense advances?   ____   ____   ____

10. If the answer to the above question is "yes," what are the limits for expected categories of expenses?   ____ ____ ____

11. Does the company provide credit cards for company-related expenses?
    a. Visa, AMEX, Diners, etc.?   ____ ____ ____
    b. Oil company card for auto expenses?   ____ ____ ____
    c. Air Travel card?   ____ ____ ____
    d. If an Air Travel card is furnished, is its use limited to the employee's business travel cost only or is it un-limited? For example, pur-chasing fare for other company employees and similar authorized expenses? ____ ____ ____
    e. What class of air travel is allowed?
       1. For business trips of two hours or less: ____ ____ ____
       2. For business trips of more than two hours: ____ ____ ____
       3. For vacations and home leave: ____ ____ ____

12. Is the employee expected to use his or her own funds for company business expense as a routine practice?   ____ ____ ____

13. Will the employee's immediate superior be the sole person approving expense reports?   ____ ____ ____

14. If the answer to the above question is "no," then who else is involved in the approval process?   ____ ____ ____

15. How quickly are expense
reports approved, processed
by accounting, and the emp-
loyee reimbursed? _____   _____   _____

F. Legal considerations

1. Has the company been sued
by employee(s), indigenous or
expatriate, and if so, why
and what were results? _____   _____   _____

2. Has the company been sued
by clients and if so, why
and what were results? _____   _____   _____

3. Does the company have an
in-house lawyer or legal advisor
or do they use a consulting firm? _____   _____   _____

G. Safety and security

1. Does the company have
a good safety record? _____   _____   _____

2. What is the company's safety
standing in its industry? _____   _____   _____

3. Has the company had many
insurance claims for per-
sonnel injuries? _____   _____   _____

4. Are the company's offices,
equipment, and job sites clean
and well maintained? _____   _____   _____

5. Are safety signs numerous
and prominently displayed? _____   _____   _____

6. Are employees observed
wearing/using safety equipment
(where appropriate)? _____   _____   _____

7. Are (will) security guards (be)
furnished day and night at the
employee's residence? _____   _____   _____

8. If the answer to the above question is "yes," will these guards be professional military or police?   ____   ____   ____

H. The compensation package offered

1. Base salary offered   ____   ____   ____
2. Performance incentive:
   a. Is it easily calculated?   ____   ____   ____
   b. How much or within what range (in U.S. dollars) is the incentive expected to be?   ____   ____   ____
   c. Is its payment subject to the performance of others?   ____   ____   ____
   d. When or how often paid?   ____   ____   ____
   e. Does the employee set goals within guidelines provided by management or are goals set by others?   ____   ____   ____
   f. Are incentives available to all employees or just a selected few?   ____   ____   ____
   g. What is the local tax impact on incentives?   ____   ____   ____
   h. Are stock options available?   ____   ____   ____
   i. If stock options are available, what are the terms and how often available?   ____   ____   ____
   j. Can income be deferred to reduce personal tax burden?   ____   ____   ____
   k. Is there a company investment program?   ____   ____   ____
   l. Is there a company profit-sharing program?   ____   ____   ____
   m. Is there a company pension plan available to the employee?   ____   ____   ____
3. Insurance
   a. Life insurance terms, amount(s) and who pays?   ____   ____   ____

      b.   Accidental death and dismemberment insurance terms, amount, and who pays?   ____   ____   ____

      c.   Loss of income insurance terms, amount, and who pays?   ____   ____   ____

      d.   Medical insurance benefits, amounts, and who pays?   ____   ____   ____

      e.   Dental insurance benefits, amounts, and who pays?   ____   ____   ____

      f.   Sick leave policy   ____   ____   ____

      g.   What is the overall monetary value of the benefits package as a percentage base pay?   ____   ____   ____

      h.   What is the overall monetary value of the benefits package as a percentage of total pay? ____   ____   ____

      i.   Has the benefits package as a percentage of base pay been steadily rising or falling over the past five years?   ____   ____   ____

      j.   Is the benefits package expected to increase or decrease in the future?   ____   ____   ____

 4. Accommodations—temporary

      a.   Are (will) temporary accommodations (be) acceptable?   ____   ____   ____

 5. Accommodations—permanent

      a.   Is the allowance for accommodations adequate to obtain the quality of accommodations acceptable to the employee?   ____   ____   ____

      b.   Are acceptable accommodations even available?   ____   ____   ____

      c.   Is the neighborhood where most employees live adequate or barely acceptable?   ____   ____   ____

d. Can accommodations be leased for my entire stay or will I be required to move one or more times? ___ ___ ___

e. Will the employee have the opportunity to move to a new or different location if the first accommodation chosen (or its location) proves to be not acceptable? ___ ___ ___

f. Will accommodations be furnished or unfurnished? ___ ___ ___

g. If furnished, what is the style and quality of furniture? ___ ___ ___

h. Are drapes and curtains furnished? ___ ___ ___

i. Are appliances furnished and acceptable in size, etc.?
    1. Stove? ___ ___ ___
    2. Oven? ___ ___ ___
    3. Refrigerator? ___ ___ ___
    4. Freezer? ___ ___ ___

j. Air-conditioning (defined as cooling *and* heating, where applicable)
    1. All rooms or just the bedrooms? ___ ___ ___
    2. Are ceiling fans installed in all rooms? ___ ___ ___

6. Automobiles (two—one for business and one for family use)

a. Are company and family automobile types and age typical for the employee's position? ___ ___ ___

b. Are the automobiles equivalent to the types, quality, etc. provided to staff and clients of a similar status? ___ ___ ___

    c. How often replaced with
new?   ____   ____   ____

    d. Automobile fuel,
lube, other service and
maintenance—who pays?   ____   ____   ____

    e. Are automobile insurance
types of coverage and
amounts adequate?   ____   ____   ____

    f. Is there a mobile or cellular
telephone in each
automobile?   ____   ____   ____

    g. Does each automobile have
a radio, tape or CD player, and
an adequate sound system?   ____   ____   ____

    h. Can the automobile assigned
for business use be used for
personal use as well?   ____   ____   ____

7. Vacations
   a. How many *working days*
   or *working hours* vacation
   given each year?   ____   ____   ____
   b. Is this paid vacation?   ____   ____   ____
   c. Is return air fare to and
   from point of origin provided
   during vacations?   ____   ____   ____
   d. What holidays (in addition
   to vacation) are allowed?   ____   ____   ____

10

Sources of Information
for the Employee

Acquisition of essential reference material should be a priority for anyone considering overseas employment, regardless of the country. Some of the first questions asked will be, "where is the country (and city or village) where we will be living, what other countries are nearby, how far will we be from home?" and similar considerations.

An obvious first source for answers is any good encyclopedia. Encyclopedias not only provide maps, but they also provide the history and other important information about the country. In some cases borders and names of countries may have recently changed; therefore, even the most up-to-date encyclopedia may list the country under its old name.

The embassy or nearest consulate office of the country in question is another source of information. Since these offices normally have publications for both business and tourist interests, it's advisable to ask for both when calling or writing. Remember that these documents are meant to promote commerce and may not provide all of the needed information before accepting an overseas assignment.

Any good bookstore in most medium-to-large cities will have an assortment of maps from which to choose. If an acceptable map can't be found in a local bookstore, then a map catalog should be obtained. One such catalog that is a must in anyone's library is *The Map Catalog, Every Kind of Map and Chart on Earth and Even Some Above*, published by Tilden Press[R] Inc. This catalog not only describes various types of maps, but it also lists the names of companies and addresses where they can be obtained. However, the catalog is primarily aimed at the United States and Canadian markets, and it is not especially helpful for persons from other countries, unless it is convenient to order through the North American stores or suppliers listed.

Michelin™ produces maps as well as their famous "Green" and "Red" guides. The "Green" guides contain detail maps and provide a wealth of historical information and suggestions on what to see and where to go; the "Red" guides list a range of restaurants and hotels including such details as level of quality, costs, and similar. Unfortunately, the majority of these publications cover developed and few developing countries. A current list of available Michelin™ maps and guides can be obtained through most bookstores.

The Falk Plan™ maps are very good and come in a foldout book form that is convenient, especially when riding in an automobile. These are available for most principal cities in Europe and some principal cities in developing countries. If not available through a local bookstore, write Falk-Verlag™ GmbH, 2000 Hamburg 1, Burchardstr. 8, Germany, for the nearest source.

Numerous travel guides are available. Among the most popular are those produced or edited by Eugene Fodor™ and Arthur Frommer™. APA Productions™ publishes a series of Insight Guides™ that are available for many developing countries, and very good.

An obvious need is a good phrase book for the local language. The Berlitz™ books have always been popular. Again, most bookstores carry these (or similar) books or can order them. If the language is not well known outside of the country or region, then the embassy or consulate may be able to recommend a book and how to obtain it. For the person seriously interested in fitting into the culture, language tapes should also be obtained, if available.

Medical reference books are a necessity. The following are available in the United States:

AARP Pharmacy Service, *Prescription Drug Handbook*. The Editorial Advisory Board, Nancy J. Olins, M.A., Editorial Coordinator; Glenview, Il.: American Association of Retired Persons, Scott Foresman and Company, (latest edition). This is published primarily for members of AARP but is a valuable book for anyone.

American Medical Association, *The American Medical Association Family Medical Guide*. Edited by Jeffrey R.M. Kunz, M.D. and Asher J. Finkel, M.D.; New York, N.Y.: Random House, Inc., 1987.

Consumer Guide, *Family Medical & Health Guide*. With Ira J. Chasnoff, M.D., Jeffrey W. Ellis, M.D., and Zachary S. Fainman, M.D.; Lincolnwood, Il.: Publications International, (latest edition).

Consumer Guide, *Prescription Drugs*. Drug consultants: Donald Autio, M.S., Deborah Harper Brown, Pharm.D., Jerry Frazier, Pharm.D., Maureen Garrity, B.S., Cheryl Nunn, Pharm.D., Ladia Cheng, Pharm.D., and Phillip Nowakowski, Pharm.D.; Lincolnwood, Il.: Publications International, (latest edition).

Merck & Co., Inc., *The Merck Manual of Diagnosis and Therapy*. Robert Berkow, M.D., Editor-in-Chief; Rahway, New Jersey: Merck Sharp & Dohme Research Laboratories, (latest edition).

Simon, Gilbert I., Sc.D. and Silverman, Harold M., Pharm. D., *The Pill Book*. Bert Stern, Producer, Lawrence D. Chilnick, Editor-in Chief; New York, N.Y.: Bantam Books, (latest edition).

U.S. Department of Health, Education, and Welfare, Public Health Services Administration Bureau of Medical Services, *The Ship's Medicine Chest and Medical Aid at Sea*. Prepared by the staff of the Bureau of Medical Services, U.S. Public Health Service; Washington D.C.: U.S. Government Printing Office, (latest edition).

It is sometimes possible to obtain good medical reference material from technical bookstores in developing countries, especially if a medical school is nearby. Typically, these books are locally (or regionally) printed through a license agreements with major publishing houses in developed countries. Although the quality of paper and other features may not be the same as in the original publication, most expatriates should find them adequate.

Information on tax planning can be obtained from international accounting firms such as KPMG Peat Marwick™. They have guides to business and individual taxes in most developed and developing countries.

Daily newspapers from the city where the employee will be living are a good source of information. If time permits, the employee should obtain a subscription for one or more months prior to accepting employment. Besides getting the flavor of local activities and politics, advertisements by real estate, grocery, and other concerns will provide an idea of what's available and what the cost of living will be. The name and address of important newspapers can usually be obtained from the country's embassy or nearest consulate office. Ask for the Commercial Section or Attache. If employment negotiations are already in progress, the prospective employer may be willing to obtain a subscription for the employee.

Other newspapers, one or more of which are typically subscribed to by expatriates, are: *The Financial Times, The International Herald Tribune,* and *The Wall Street Journal.* Financial Times Magazines publishes a monthly magazine especially for British expatriates, called *Resident Abroad.* A subscription is highly recommended, even if you are not a British citizen. Contact Financial Times Magazines, Subscription Department, P.O. Box 461, Bromley, BR2 9WP, England, for details.

Trade organizations are another good source of information. An example in the United States is the local chapter of the American Chamber of Commerce. They should be able to provide the name and address of their corresponding organization in the country in question, if there is one. Such organizations typically compile statistics on business activities as well as on cost of living surveys. Occasionally, they may publish special situation reports on specific industries or other topics of interest to the business community.

Other similar organizations exist. Usually, the name includes the developing and developed country followed by "Chamber of Commerce," "Commercial Development Organization," or similar organizations. An example would be "The Arab-American Chamber of Commerce." The names of these organizations can usually be found in the telephone directories of major cities in developed countries or through the country's embassy or nearest consulate office. Membership in such an organization is a good method of developing a network of contacts with both native and expatriate members.

Documentary-type books can provide current and historical background, where such books have been written for a particular country or region. For example, Alan Moorehead's *The White Nile* (London: Penguin Books, 1973) describes the conditions and activities in Central and East Africa during the mid-1800s to the turn of the century. A library search will reveal other similar books about other areas or countries.

11

Matchmaking or Back to Basics

While the information presented in previous chapters is aimed at achievement of the purpose and goal stated in the Preface, this final chapter will review some basic fundamentals that influence the relationship between employers and employees in any employment situation. These are as important, if not more so, in achieving the benefits both desire from the experience. If both understand, agree with, and practice these fundamentals, the relationship will have a better chance of success.

Fundamentals

For the employee to be *effective* in his or her work (no matter how simple and small or complicated and large the assignment may be), there must be a foundation of capabilities and resources in place. There must also be an understanding between employee and employer about the limits and uses of these. In this chapter these concepts are divided into the following categories:

- The employee's body of knowledge.
- The availability of resources.
- The availability of time.
- Management's delegation of authority.
- Management's and the employee's leadership abilities.
- The method of performance measurement.
- The employee's understanding of his or her assignment.

The degree to which these are understood and satisfied will have an impact on the probability of success of the employer/employee relationship; this can be thought of as *fundamental* to the success of the relationship.

The Employee's "Body of Knowledge"

To begin, the employee must have the formal education, special training, experience, and the emotional and mental competence necessary to do the work assigned, if the work is to be performed in a professional manner. This does not mean that the employee must have dealt with the *exact* type of assignment, but that the employee has a demonstrated history of successfully carrying out similar assignments in the same or a related craft, department, or industry.

For example, a secretary with experience in the international Sales Department of a pump manufacturing company could be expected to assimilate the differences and produce immediate results in the same department of a valve manufacturer. However, the secretary may not be able to adapt to a secretarial job in the Personnel Department, since there is a difference in the interests, pace, routine, and mentality of the two groups. An engineer with experience in designing self-propelled, oil-field service boats could quickly adapt to designing flat-deck cargo barges, but would probably require more time to produce results if taking a new job designing aircraft structures.

Therefore, the more familiar an employee is with an area of technology or business, its people and jargon, regulatory codes and standards, contractual and legal aspects, typical problems and typical solutions, things to avoid and things to do, day-to-day decisions that must be made, and the work *environment*; the more effective he or she should be in helping the employer achieve goals. These factors are sometimes referred to as the employee's *body of knowledge*; namely, the total of the employee's capabilities that can be applied to an assignment.

Resources

The *resources* needed by the employee to carry out the assignment must also be available. These must be of sufficient quantity and quality to support the employee's decisions and actions. A chef, for example, may have clear authority over the kitchen. However, if the kitchen is equipped poorly or the equipment doesn't work, if there is insufficient staff or lack of the ingredients needed to prepare the menu, and if there are no funds at hand to repair equipment or make the other resources available, then the chef cannot be expected to produce to the best of his or her ability.

It is one thing to dream of owning a fashionable and profitable restaurant, yet it is another to have the capital required to fulfill that dream. The quantity and quality of resources (e.g., people, cash, facilities, machinery, raw materials) available must be within the limitations set by the owner when contemplating the type and size of the business he or she does (or desires) to own. At the same time, the owner must set these limitations within practical or realistic minimums through accurate assessment of the competition and industry standards. Alternately, the owner must have some copyright or technical advantage over the competition, which he or she is confident will produce the anticipated results with a reduction in the normal level of resources.

Related to this is the environment in which the employee must work. It is unrealistic for the employer to expect contemporary standards of efficiency and production when the employee's work station is drab, congested, noisy, not clean; when the equipment is poor, or when other similar factors exist that are detrimental to employee efficiency and motivation. In other words, if the employer is perceived not to care, then the employee is unlikely to demonstrate a level of concern and ambition greater than those depended upon to lead.

Time

The term *time* is used in the *real* sense and not in the abstract. There is no alternate factor that can somehow replace or speed up time. Good planning, definition of authority, and effective use of resources can cause more to be accomplished in a given unit of time, but time itself will not be changed.

For example, it is obvious that a certain minimum amount of time is required to plan and prepare an acceptable menu in any restaurant. While some food can be prepared ahead of the arrival of customers, certain items can only be prepared when it is known what the customer wants. The exception is the cafeteria where the entire menu is (generally) prepared ahead of opening time. Except in the cafeteria (or "Today's Special" in other restaurants), it is unrealistic for a customer to expect his or her meal to be delivered *instantly*. If the customer orders the meal and immediately demands to see the chef to find out why it isn't served, then getting served will likely take longer, since the chef can't be in the kitchen looking after the preparation of the customer's meal if he or she is standing next to the customer in the dining room. A parallel to this is that some trees must grow for several years before they begin to bear fruit. If these trees are pulled from the ground every day to see if the roots are growing, it is logical that the trees will never produce fruit.

A new employee must also have time to adapt to a new environment, must get to know the personalities and capabilities of the people, and must understand the philosophy and goals of the employer. Depending upon the employee's maturity and recent past experience in a similar environment, such adaptation may be quickly achieved or protracted.

How quickly the employee becomes effective in the job is not only related to the employee's body of knowledge, skills, and personality; but it is also related to how well the company is organized and administered, how well the new employee's authority and the authority of those with whom the employee must interface are understood and the availability of the required resources, and how well these aspects of the employer's business are conveyed and understood by the employee.

Delegation of Authority

In a business having more than one employee, authority has to be delegated if resources are going to be used efficiently and profitably. Concurrent with the delegation of authority are the limitations placed upon that authority. Having *authority* means that the employee can make decisions concerning those persons and things (the resources including budgets), that come within the employee's authority. Once adequate authority has been delegated to the employee, the employee then becomes *responsible* for the use of assigned resources and the results of the actions taken to achieve stated goals.

It doesn't work the other way. In other words, an employee is not assigned responsibility without the authority to take the actions needed to control the resources and outcome of the work assigned. If adequate authority is delegated and the necessary resources made available, then the employee becomes responsible for the results of his or her actions. If adequate authority is not delegated and the needed resources not made available, then the employee cannot logically be responsible for achieving a level of quality, completeness, and professionalism that could otherwise be achieved if the missing components had been made available.

In delegating authority, care must be taken to avoid two or more people having the same level of authority for the same job or having jobs within the company that grossly overlap each other. Where overlapping or unclear demarcation exists, the effect is demoralizing to the employees involved and costly to the employer. Although there must be communications and shared responsibility between persons, groups, departments, and divisions of the company, the interface between these entities must be clearly understood. This does not mean that there shouldn't be competition between individuals or groups within the company; only that such competition should result in a positive benefit to the employer, not destructive to employee initiative or wasteful to the employer's resources.

To illustrate, a chef in a large restaurant cannot be expected to serve good meals to customers if he or she does not have the authority to choose the kitchen staff and the menu, select and buy the ingredients, and have direct control over the preparation and cooking of the food. If the chef's supervisor insists on selecting the ingredients, arbitrarily instructs the chef to alter the recipes, gives instructions to the kitchen staff that conflict with those of the chef and, in general, disrupts the kitchen routine, then the chef is not really in control and cannot be held responsible for the outcome.

Leadership

The fifth fundamental is leadership. Leadership is the ability to provide direction. To achieve this, the leader must fulfill the functions of leadership which include planning, initiating, controlling, supporting, informing, and monitoring and providing feed back. Both employer and employee must understand and insure that these functions are being fulfilled within their respective areas of authority. A leader must be able to motivate people to a high level of achievement and positive attitude. This is done by demonstrating how they can use their skills to achieve company, group, and individual goals.

Leadership ability begins with a basic understanding of what motivates people, a genuine interest in their ideas, their need to achieve, and their welfare (both individually and as a group). Leadership is not necessarily related to popularity. Subordinates must sense that they are being treated fairly and intelligently, that the company's objectives are worthy, and that employees can expect adequate verbal and material reward for their effort. Every individual must enjoy the type of work the company does and undertake his or her part enthusiastically. In other words, given a suitable environment and leadership that fulfills the above functions, employees will be self-motivated.

Good leadership involves *guiding* people, not doing their work for them or telling them how to do it. Good leadership conveys the results to be achieved and does not *control* people as an end in itself. Simply controlling people may satisfy the egocentric needs of a particular supervisor, manager, or executive, but it does not improve the efficiency of the individual or the profitability of an organization.

Control of the results (and the people involved) is gained through the process of planning in which the people who must produce the results are part of the planning and decision-making process. In this way each person can see what part he or she must play and how the effort of each person fits into the whole. Control is achieved because each person has an objective, defined resources, and a schedule and budget to accomplish the objective. Each person involved in the decision-making process must "buy into" the desired results and feel responsible for the outcome. In this way the person is motivated to do his or her part. Positive competition results as the employees involved try to accomplish their objectives in less than scheduled time and under budget, thus pushing others to do the same. Cooperation is necessary between team members because each must support and receive support from the other team members.

To achieve the desired results, management must be realistic in setting objectives, providing the resources, and establishing schedules. If management's expectations are, at the outset, grossly unrealistic to employees, then there is little motivation for the individual or group to excel. The expected rewards must be visible, not out of sight. Management's plans or expectations must also not be viewed as an insult to the employees' intelligence.

Performance Measurement

The performance of each person, department, or group in a company must be measured fairly and accurately. An excellent method of doing this is through customer feedback. A *customer* is any client, individual, department, or group in need of information or some other support that the employee is capable of providing. The employee is also a customer of some other individual, department, or group. Performance is measured by the quality and timeliness of service or support each customer receives. Some examples of *quality* service or support follow:

- A company's engineering department consistently delivered material requisitions to the purchasing department that were complete, accurate, and organized so that they were easily understood. These were always received by purchasing in time to insure delivery of the material on or before the dates needed.

- The Production Department of a certain manufacturer was receiving inconsistent cost information from accounting. The reports were also arriving too late for significant corrective action to be taken to control costs. A new head of accounting was hired who not only understood accounting principles, but also how to work with people. Shortly thereafter, the Accounting Department met with manufacturing to determine what cost information was needed by manufacturing and on what schedule. A cost accounting and reporting system was set up to meet these needs. An overall production cost savings of eight percent was achieved as a result.

- An employee was going overseas and he would be distant from his bank back home. He set up automatic payments with the bank for mortgage and other monthly bills. He sent a memo to his employer's Payroll Department requesting that they deposit his monthly check in his account at the bank. The Payroll Department analyzed the time required to get his check deposited in his bank on time to ensure that his automatic payments wouldn't create an overdraw situation.

- Accidents do happen. One month the UPS on the payroll department computer didn't catch a spike and the payroll data were lost. Within 48 hours the system was back on line and the payroll complete. In the meantime, the payroll manager's secretary contacted the employee's bank directly and explained the delay. The bank agreed to make the automatic payments on the employee's behalf without delay at no cost to the employee.

- A company salesman landed a really big job. In the process he meticulously scrutinized every aspect of the deal; namely, the specifications, delivery dates, client report requirements, how and when his company would get paid, and all other aspects. He prepared a report detailing how the deal was going to work, who was to do what and when (including any points that still needed to be worked out with the client), and the plan for doing this. His work was so complete that engineering, purchasing, and manufacturing had no problems filling the order on time. All internal groups were (and still are) pleased with the salesman's work—and so is the client.

- Due to the company's work load, the senior and middle management staff were in the office long hours including most Saturdays and Sundays. The chief executive officer recognized that this schedule was hard on the employees' families as well. There wasn't much he could do about the physical separation, but he did determine that there were two services he could provide (at a nominal cost to the company) that would show his appreciation for the effort of the staff and reduce at least some of each staff member's responsibilities at home.

   He first contracted an auto maintenance company to have someone at the office each day to wash and service staff members' cars—both company furnished and personally owned. In this way each staff member had a clean vehicle in which to ride and never had to worry about stopping to check fluid levels, the tires, and so forth. However, each employee did have to pay for fuel, oil, lube, and filters for personal autos.

   Secondly, he arranged for the services of a professional company to maintain the lawn and shrubbery at each employee's home. This was provided at no cost on a weekly basis during the spring and summer and twice a month during the fall and winter.

   In addition to these services, he arranged a picnic-type lunch one afternoon each weekend at the office. He had the meat courses brought in by a caterer; each family brought a dish to complete the menu. In this way each employee was able to spend at least some time with his or her spouse and children and got to know the other staff and their families better as well.

   The staff motivation resulting from the concern displayed by the chief executive officer resulted in a high level of team work and overall performance. This company became one of the most successful in its industry.

No one (no matter what their position, title, or family affiliations) can be exempt from an analysis of their performance as a provider of quality service or support. This concept must be consistently applied. Feedback concerning quality performance is as important to employee motivation, if not more so, than reports of negative performance.

Employee's Understanding of His or Her Assignment

In addition to management that understands and fulfills the functions of good leadership, the most basic tool that the employee must have is an understanding of what he or she is expected to do; that is, what part is going to be played in the company. This is normally provided in the form of a *job description*. There are numerous formats for job descriptions. The one provided in attachment V should be adequate for most employment situations.

A Closing Comment

As mentioned earlier, the author is not an attorney and has prepared this guide based on personal experience and information passed on to the author and alleged to be the experiences of others. This book is not represented nor intended to be professional legal advice. Anyone employing or assigning an expatriate employee for or to a job outside the employee's country of origin or, any person considering such employment or assignment should seek professional advice from an attorney (preferably one experienced in overseas employment contracts), an accounting firm with offices in the country in question, and an insurance consultant. The purpose of the book is to improve communications between employer and employee by exploring and discussing many aspects of such employment. The primary goal is for the parties to have a clear understanding of the implications of such employment so that both will realize the benefits each expects from the experience. If employers and employees are better informed as a result of this book, then its purpose and goal will have been achieved.